OPP

Recreation
and Leisure
Careers

OPPORTUNITIES

in

Recreation and Leisure Careers

REVISED EDITION

CLAYNE JENSEN AND JAY H. NAYLOR

REVISED EDITION BY NATALIA BUTA AND AMY DECKER

McGraw·Hill

New York   Chicago   San Francisco   Lisbon   London   Madrid   Mexico City
Milan   New Delhi   San Juan   Seoul   Singapore   Sydney   Toronto

1 2 3 4 5 6 7 8 9 0   DOC/DOC   0 9 8 7 6 5

ISBN 0-07-144854-3

Interior design by Rattray Design

McGraw-Hill books are available at special quantity discounts to use as premiums and sales promotions, or for use in corporate training programs. For more information, please write to the Director of Special Sales, Professional Publishing, McGraw-Hill, Two Penn Plaza, New York, NY 10121-2298. Or contact your local bookstore.

This book is printed on acid-free paper.

I would like to dedicate this revised edition to my brother, Florin, who never stopped encouraging and supporting me in making my dreams become a reality. I thank my parents who understood and believed in my goals. I am the person I am today because they nurtured my ambition. It is with great appreciation that I acknowledge the faculty of the RPL Department. They provided me the opportunity to study at Central Michigan University. Thank you all!

—Natalia Buta

Life is made up of experiences that are never solely ours. They are shared with every person we come into contact with, because each has an impact on who we are. It goes without saying that my mentors, my friends, my fiancé, and my family lend the most to who I am today. But there are three individuals who, on a daily basis, teach me about the person I wish to become. Randi, Kevin, and Maddie's love, energy, and curiosity are the greatest source of inspiration, and it is to them that I dedicate this revision.

—Amy Decker

CONTENTS

Association. Canadian Association for Health, Physical Education, Recreation, and Dance. Employee Services Management Association. National Recreation and Park Association.

Foreword

We invite you to explore the exciting and remarkably diverse career opportunities that are available in the profession of recreation and leisure services. There has never been a more exciting time to become involved. Today we are increasingly a leisure-oriented society. The average full-time employee works fewer than forty hours a week. A third of our time is spent in leisure, and a third of our income goes toward leisure pursuits. One-third of our land is donated to leisure and recreation, and more than two-thirds of Americans perceive that their leisure is of equal or greater importance to them than their work. Increasingly, we are apt to measure the quality of our lives by the satisfactions derived from our leisure experiences. As a result, jobs in this field are plentiful, and continued growth in career opportunities can be expected in the next decades.

Professional careers in recreation and leisure services offer challenging, meaningful, and highly rewarding opportunities in human services. Whether your interests are in working with children, teens, adults, or seniors, the settings to engage people are abundant. Opportunities are found within outdoor, community, commercial, military, correctional, and therapeutic recreation. Whether it is high-adventure or natural resource management, league sports or community centers, cultural or performing arts, professional sports venues or special events, pediatric hospitals or residential rehabilitation, military bases or state/federal correctional facilities, recreation and leisure services offer job possibilities that fit you.

We invite you to consider a career in the profession of recreation and leisure services. You will have the satisfaction of enjoying your work and an opportunity to make unique and significant contributions to the quality of life of those you serve.

Good luck with your career.

Roger L. Coles, Ed.D.
Department Chair, Recreation
Central Michigan University

PREFACE

LEISURE OCCUPATIONS ARE among the most rapidly growing vocations in America. The recreation industry has been and is currently preparing for a leisure-oriented society. The field of recreational leadership has become a well-established profession. Consequently, there has been an upsurge in career opportunities and career preparation programs in leisure-related fields.

Serving an industry that annually exceeds $150 billion in expenditures, trained workers in a variety of occupations are involved in the provision of leisure services. Visualize, for example, the variety of jobs and the number of people who are involved in the design and production of sporting and recreation equipment, the provision of all sorts of recreation services, facility planning and construction, program planning, and direct recreation leadership. Further, commercial entertainment establishments, travel agencies, professional sports organizations, outdoor recreation producers, and many other such services are very much a part of the exploding leisure market. Indeed, leisure services, in total, employ millions of people in commercial, community, therapeutic, outdoor, and hospitality settings.

Since it would be impractical to cover all of the leisure occupations, the content of this book is limited to the recreation and park profession within the United States and Canada and certain closely related fields. Unlike many areas of employment that face the threat of diminishing importance because of technology and automation, this interesting occupational field will offer expanding opportunities in both the near- and long-term future.

Acknowledgments

We would like to extend our appreciation to Roger Coles and Peggy Gisler for the opportunity to revise this book. Their unfailing trust and guidance has been invaluable. We are indebted to the authors and previous editors who invested their time and energy into the text. Their insight proves to be not only a great contribution to the industry but to our professional development as well. Also, our thanks goes to Dean Pybus, who has been a constant driving force and mentor in our work.

1

RECREATION FOR
A NEW GENERATION

Leisure is the best of all possessions.

—Socrates

THANKS TO MODERN technology, increased vacation time, flexible work schedules, and early retirement, many people are able to enjoy recreation and leisure time now more than in any other period in our history. Not only have the philosophies and possibilities of recreation changed, but people are also spending their leisure time participating in activities that their grandparents would never even have dreamed could exist. New trends like in-line skating, snowboarding, and hang gliding emerge continuously.

What do you enjoy doing during your leisure time? Housework? Doing research at the library? Grocery shopping? Not on your life! When you think of how you want to spend your leisure time, you usually think of doing recreational activities like hiking, golf, tennis, and camping. In the minds of most people, recreation and the use of leisure time are synonymous. However, it is important to recognize that there are many uses of leisure time that are not recreative.

The word *recreation* is derived from the Latin word *recreare*, which means to create anew, restore, refresh. The *Merriam-Webster Online* dictionary further defines the term as "the refreshment of strength and spirits." Recreation is essentially a "renewing" experience—an invigorating change from work and the daily routine.

If we accept the idea that recreation actually recreates the participant, then many so-called recreation pursuits are not recreation at all. They are only amusers, time fillers, and time wasters, some of which fatigue rather than rejuvenate, "decreate" rather than recreate, and actually deprive participants of enrichment opportunities vital to their development and fulfillment. The popular terminology for this is called "purple recreation." Based on perception, activities like gambling, substance abuse, graffiti, gang activities, and pornography do not embody the essence of the definition of recreation.

In his book, *Philosophy of Recreation and Leisure*, J. B. Nash added meaning to the quality concept of recreation by placing different kinds of pursuits into a hierarchy on the basis of their potential value to the individual and society. Figure 1 is a modified version of Nash's original interpretation.

The deeper meaning of recreation goes beyond amusement and hobby. It includes activities of the highest order of creative, cultural, and civic values that enrich our lives and elevate the tone of society. Clear understanding of this broader concept among recreation professionals and community leaders is critical because it is a fundamental concept that is already being forgotten.

Figure 1 Quality Concepts in the Pursuit of Recreation

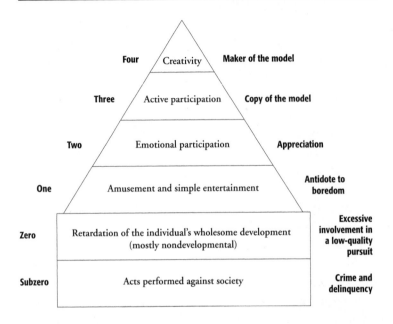

The term *recreation* implies that the participant is recreated physically, psychologically, spiritually, or mentally; that he or she becomes refreshed and enriched; that he or she is revitalized and more ready to cope with the routines and trials of life. True recreation is clearly distinguished from simple amusements and time fillers because true recreation provides an experience of quality to the participant.

Recreational activities take many forms and must be suited to an individual's particular needs and interests. People enjoy fishing, skiing, singing, photography, dancing, playing a guitar, swimming, or going to a good play; nevertheless, one person's recreation may be another's drudgery. Building a boat, for example, can be an ideal leisure activity to one person, whereas to another it would be work.

Even for one individual, an activity that is recreational at one time or under certain conditions does not always yield satisfaction that makes it recreation. Sometimes a person feels like playing golf or participating in a square dance group; at other times he or she prefers a very different form of involvement. When a person is physically exhausted, there is little need for vigorous physical recreation. When mentally or emotionally fatigued, a person is not attracted to activities that require heavy concentration.

Recreation usually takes the form of diversion and helps to bring one's life into balance. To some, the park is a place to play. To others, it is for beauty, meditation, and the study of nature. An important task of leisure professionals is to identify the needs and interests of different people and to supply facilities, programs, and leadership that will be appealing and satisfying.

Recreation is often determined by the characteristics of being active and interactive. Sometimes looking and listening is inappropriately labeled as recreation. Very often this kind of involvement is no more than a time filler; however, there is a level of being a spectator that may be creative. When an individual goes to a concert, views a painting, hears a pianist, observes a favorite athlete, or sees the performance or products of people in whom he or she has special interest, there may be a beneficial level of emotional participation or a creative result. The observer may say, "That's what I would like to have said," or "That is what I believe." Participating in such a manner lifts an individual to a higher level. Standing before Michelangelo's *David* or Rodin's *Thinker*, or attending a worthy performance, may cause the appreciative person to want to live better and accomplish more. Sometimes seeing and listening provides an example for the individual that results in improvement or arouses a level of appreciation. On the other hand, the danger of being a spectator is that people will simply be amused and pacified hour after hour, and this may actually destroy motivation and opportunity to do something more developmental and worthy.

The Total Recreation Experience

At first, a recreation experience may appear to be confined to the block of time during which participation actually occurs. But upon further analysis, it becomes apparent that the total experience extends far beyond the time of physical involvement. The value and usefulness of the experience may be part of a person's life long before, and remain long after, the participation itself. A total recreation experience includes the following four phases: anticipation, planning, participation, and recollection.

The anticipation phase is that time during which the person foresees the greatness of the coming event—the time of eagerly waiting for the day when the experience will become a reality. It is during this time that enthusiasm starts to develop. This phase may include the anticipation of catching a big trout, climbing a high mountain, bagging a deer, the thought of next summer's canoe trip, learning to ski, or riding horseback. Sometimes this phase occurs over an extended period of time and often stimulates some reading and study, and much conversation.

The planning phase involves the actual preparation for the coming event—gathering equipment and supplies, purchasing food, packing clothes, making travel arrangements, and other such necessary matters. If done well, this process can be a pleasant and educational experience. It teaches an individual that even the smallest detail matters within the flow and enjoyment of the event. For example, having fun with snowmobiles for a winter-weekend get-away is difficult if you forget the keys to the snowmobile on the counter at home. Planning is crucial. It helps to avoid unexpected situations, the anxiety of dealing with problems, and the distress that arises if a problem can't be solved.

The participation phase is the period of engaging in the activity for the desired duration of the event. It extends from the time of departure until the time of return. Often this phase is relatively short when compared to the other phases, and it may seem almost insignificant in terms of time. Yet it is the core around which the other three phases are built. This is the actual experience.

The recollection phase may take the form of memories, expression in oral or written form, or the displaying of pictures, slides, and movies. This phase is the thinking, telling, and showing about the experiences that have occurred. Fortunately, there is no time limit for this phase.

Sometimes anticipation, planning, and recollection are more exciting than the participation itself, but it takes all four phases to make the recreational experience complete. None of the four phases should be downplayed in terms of its potential contributions.

Dealing with Misconceptions

Along with the large number of books and articles that have been written during recent years on leisure and recreation, so, too, have occurred a number of misconceptions. It is important to identify these misconceptions and try to correct or avoid them.

1. It is often thought that recreation is strictly the antithesis of work. This is a misconception. It is true that for many people the hours of employment are repetitive, boring, and exhausting. Today

relatively few people find recreation in their work, but there are some individuals who do.

2. Leisure time and recreation are frequently treated as though they are essentially the same or inseparable. This is not totally correct. It is true that in most instances, opportunities for recreation are confined to leisure hours. Therefore, recreation is primarily a leisure time activity. However, not all leisure time is spent in recreational pursuits. Much of it is spent or occupied with activities that do not have recreative results. Leisure time can be filled either with true recreation or with low-grade amusers, time wasters, or "decreative" activities.

3. Some people stress the concept that recreation must be earned by doing useful work. This would imply that recreation is not essential in and of itself; instead, it is a recuperative interlude between periods of work. They fail to recognize the significant nature and vital purpose of recreation—a desirable state of being.

4. Some see recreation only as therapeutic in nature, as a means of solving or alleviating personal and community problems. The fact is, recreation doesn't always contribute to the physical relief of burdens; however, it is likely to bring greater mental and emotional satisfaction if it also contributes to the individual's personal development and to the betterment of his or her community.

5. To think of recreation as specific activities is a misconception. Recreation should be thought of as a result, not simply an activity. Even though certain activities frequently yield pleasurable experiences to a large number of people, they are merely a means of achieving recreation.

6. Another misconception is that recreation, unlike education, is essentially without purpose or discipline. This misunderstanding occurs because recreation is identified with relaxation or pleasurable involvement. In many forms of recreation there is a high degree

of concentration, physical exertion, and mental application. Some forms are stimulating and enriching, while other forms are keenly challenging and press the participants almost to their limits. These forms of recreation certainly result in individual development.

A Challenge for You

Parks and recreation professionals are facing many challenges as they progress in an ever-changing society. Their job is to provide people with opportunities for relief from the stressful environments they live in. They play a vital role in people living healthier and happier lives. As communities become more diverse, parks and recreation professionals must continually re-examine their approach to recreation so they are able to meet the changing needs of the citizens they serve. Not only will they be challenged by youth in at-risk environments and individuals wanting high-risk adventures such as bungee jumping, skydiving, and mountain climbing, but they will also be challenged to keep up with technological advances. Computers are no longer the strict domain of accountants and engineers. Computers are in schools and grocery stores and play a complex role in park and recreation facilities.

The emphasis on computer literacy continues to increase in parks and recreation. Employees working in these fields must be able to use computers and statistical techniques to assess, plan, and evaluate. The changing times surrounding the parks and recreation professionals look bright, provided that they place no boundaries or limitations on the challenges they will face in their profession.

They must also face the fact that another basic problem associated with increased leisure time is that it does not guarantee an improved society or individual. Rather, it requires the making of choices; and to ensure wise choices, the recreation and leisure fields must provide both adequate education and good leadership. Leaders in the recreation and park field must help to provide people with positive alternatives and an adequate background to make the right choices.

Americans have not yet proved that abundant leisure can be used beneficially. The "leisure era" is still in the development stage, and the outcome is certainly in question. There are some bright aspects of the leisure trend caused by perceptive and responsible people who have stood ready to add quality and meaning to life through challenging and enriching leisure pursuits. However, there is also a segment of the population that has seriously abused its newfound treasure, even to the point of using it for pursuits that are degrading. Society must deal with the fundamental problem that abundant opportunity for leisure is inherently neither good nor bad, but it has tremendous potential for either. Leisure activities simply provide new opportunities for people to make choices.

Are You Suited to the Challenge?

As a leisure professional, you must believe wholeheartedly in those opportunities. You must be someone who enjoys and understands the importance of your recreation and leisure time. In reading this book, you will be given insight if you are considering a full-time career organizing and directing activities that will meet the physical and mental needs of a diverse group of people. However, before you jump into the field, take the time to ask yourself the following questions to make sure you are really on the path of your dream career.

- Do you enjoy working with people?
- Do you enjoy the outdoor experience?

- Are you able to work with a diverse group of people?
- Do you have the ability to lead?
- Are you knowledgeable about recreational activities and equipment?
- Do you enjoy participating in athletic programs?
- Do you have the ability to help people find the recreational activity to meet their needs?
- Can you teach adults and children?
- Are you able to provide guidance and supervision in recreational activities?
- Are you a quick thinker?
- Can you handle a crisis situation?
- Can you get a diverse group of people involved in one activity?
- Do you enjoy leisure activities in all types of weather?
- Do you mind working more than forty hours a week?
- Are you flexible enough to work a diverse schedule?

If you were able to respond positively to most of these questions, then you should continue reading this book. In Chapter 2 you will learn about current occupations in the field that are needed to meet society's demands. Chapters 3 and 4 discuss the options and trends affecting employment today. Chapter 5 describes the characteristics and essential professional goals you must have for a successful career in the recreation and leisure field.

If you are really serious about finding a career in recreation and leisure, then Chapter 6 will prove invaluable because it gives information about the educational training you will need. Chapter 7 gives you tips on where to find a job. In Chapter 8 you will enjoy reading personal stories of people working in the field that you are now seriously considering.

Chapter 9 looks at some organizations that can provide you with more information about recreation and leisure careers. Many professionals suggest becoming an active member in such organizations for many reasons: They offer education, support, and networking—all of which might help enhance your career.

Chapter 10 gives you an overview of how recreation and leisure careers are keeping up with the times and what you can expect in the future. Chapter 11 covers the recreation and leisure field in Canada. Finally, the appendixes will provide you with sources for advanced schooling in recreation and leisure, professional organizations in the field, federal and state agencies, and potential employing organizations.

Opportunities for employment in parks and recreation vary greatly from one facility to another. You could work out in the field as a park ranger, be involved in the planning and programming of activities, or even work in a main office as a recreation administrator at recreation areas ranging from community park systems to national parks. All of these positions and facilities, and many more, would provide their own challenges and satisfactions for someone working in the recreation and leisure field.

2

Development of the
Recreation Profession

*How we Americans spend leisure time might seem to have little
bearing on the strength of our nation or the worth and prestige
of our free society. Yet we certainly cannot continue to thrive as
a strong and vigorous free people unless we understand and use
creatively one of our greatest resources—our leisure.*

—John F. Kennedy

THE EARLIEST CITY park in the United States was the Boston Commons, established in 1634. When in 1682 William Penn laid out
Philadelphia, he included in his plan numerous small parks and
ornamental plots. In his 1791 plan for Washington, DC, Pierre
Charles L'Enfant provided spacious public parks, squares, fountains,
walks, and broad, tree-lined avenues. Squares, commons, and village greens had become numerous in the New England states by
the early nineteenth century.

Quite separate from the city park movement, municipal recreation programming was born out of social conscience. It grew up with the settlement house, kindergarten, and youth movements that fostered the great youth agencies of the nation. Its earliest practitioners were motivated by human welfare; the social ends of human development, suppression of juvenile delinquency, informal education, cultural enrichment, health improvement, and other similar objectives were central.

Certain events of the late nineteenth century brought about the realization that there was a growing need for new and different kinds of leisure time opportunities. A rapidly changing industrialized society, along with the advancement of science, more formal education, increased population and urbanization, and changing social attitudes, had immediate effects on leisure time and its uses.

During the 1820s and 1830s, a new trend emerged when several outdoor gymnasiums were built in Massachusetts and New York. In 1853 New York City acquired Central Park—the first time any city in the United States set aside public land strictly for leisure purposes. During the second half of the century, numerous cities followed New York's example and acquired large tracts of land for parks.

The first record of anyone being employed in a leisure time occupation, other than those who planned parks, was in 1885 when several women were hired as supervisors for children's playgrounds in Boston. In 1898 New York City opened thirty-one supervised playgrounds under the direction of the State Board of Education, and, soon after that, the city moved quickly to develop a large network of playgrounds paid for and administered by the city government. Further, all schools in the city were required to have open-air playgrounds. By the end of the nineteenth century, at least fourteen American cities had made provisions for supervised public recreation facilities.

At about the same time, the settlement house movement was underway, spreading rapidly in densely populated areas. These social settlements had many of the same characteristics as today's community recreation centers.

The first metropolitan park system was established in Boston in 1892, and the first county system was organized in Essex County, New Jersey, in 1895. The New England Association of Park Superintendents (later known as the American Institute of Park Executives) was organized in 1898. By the turn of the century, the pattern for the recreation and park movement was well established.

The basis of this new movement was essentially social. Its early advocates pointed to such evils as dangerous streets, delinquency, unsanitary living conditions, child labor, congestion of cities, and lack of space for play and rest. They declared that the individual should be the center of the educational effort and that activities during leisure were important to a person's overall development.

Chicago's South Park Playground System developed during the early 1900s, and these playgrounds, with their carefully planned field houses and spacious outdoor areas, had significant influence on the recreation movement. This concept represented a milestone in the public's responsibility for facilities and paid leadership. The concept spread quickly into Rochester, Boston, and Los Angeles.

By 1906 the recreation and park movement had gained such support that at a meeting of park and playground promoters in Washington, DC, a new organization was founded—the Playground Association of America, which later became the National Recreation Association (1917), and still later the National Recreation and Park Association (1965). Joseph Lee, who was a Harvard law school graduate and wealthy philanthropist, was president of the association for twenty-seven years. Lee argued that play was a serious activity in children's social adjustment and that recreation had vital significance for everyone who wanted a meaningful life. Lee emphasized quality experiences and advocated the need for fixed goals, efficient organization, and expert leadership. He also advocated education for the wise use of leisure as the means to helping people achieve happy and creative lives.

Although they were disruptive to the development of recreation in some respects, both world wars actually contributed markedly to the movement. Men in the service were being exposed to well-organized recreational services. Further, many civilians clustered in industrial centers, where they also were exposed to facilitated recreation. Following each war, soldiers and civilians carried back to their own communities the desire to provide better-organized programs.

During the period between the two wars, the country became increasingly industrialized and highly mobile. These two characteristics had dramatic influences on the amount and kinds of leisure time activities engaged in by Americans.

Following World War II, with the American economy at its highest level in history and with the return of large numbers of soldiers and defense workers to their hometowns, practically every community of any size initiated some sort of community recreation program. In most cases the program was sponsored by the local government and supported from tax funds. It was during this period that the municipal recreation and park movement erupted into a nationwide trend.

Concurrently and subsequently, other agencies gave additional attention to people's leisure time needs. Voluntary youth-serving agencies became more concerned about the recreational needs of their members, and at industrial plants, employee recreation associations developed. The armed forces also continued to provide recreational opportunities for their members, and use of the outdoors for recreational purposes skyrocketed. During the postwar years commercial recreation enjoyed its greatest boom, and, more recently, specialized programs of recreation therapy for persons with disabilities have become popular.

Modern technology has revolutionized certain leisure time pursuits. For example boating, waterskiing, snow skiing, scuba diving, driving for pleasure, tourist travel, modern camping, video games, and numerous other forms of recreation have been influenced greatly by technological advances.

Further, television has had a significant influence through mass exposure of activities that would otherwise remain relatively unexposed. Over the past decade there have been major increases in some activities, while others have decreased. Some of the largest increases were in snowboarding, in-line skating, and step aerobics. Some of the biggest decreases were in windsurfing, tennis, and racquetball. Overall, though, more people are taking advantage of recreation activities, and the decrease in one activity is made up for with an increase in others.

Because of the steady escalation of leisure time and recreational participation, there are now numerous leisure-related job opportunities at every level of public agencies (especially the local level), in volunteer organizations, and with private and commercial enterprises. For the most part, the jobs are specialized, requiring people with certain personality characteristics and specific competencies. Because of the great variety of agencies and activities involved, there is a good chance that an interesting and challenging leisure-related occupation could await you.

Divisions of Recreation

The recreation field has been logically divided into four groups: recreation services, recreation resources, tourism, and amusement and entertainment.

The recreation services group involves leadership in organized recreational activities. This includes creating and supervising programs, planning activities, and providing leadership and instruction. These leisure time experiences take place in a variety of settings—parks, playgrounds, camps, community centers—and involve a great deal of personal interaction.

The recreation resources group includes jobs relating to the planning, development, maintenance, and protection of resources, both natural and man-made, used for leisure time activities. These jobs deal with recreational areas and facilities, and in a sense, they form a support system for recreational experiences.

The tourism group includes jobs that are related to travel for pleasure (rather than for business or duty) as well as activities for tourists. Within this group are five major components: attracting a market for tourism; providing transportation to places of interest; providing attractions for tourist participation; housing, feeding, and serving tourists; and informing people about attractions, services, facilities, and transportation, and then making the specific arrangements for them.

Developing, planning, marketing, promoting, facilitating, managing, and evaluating are areas within the amusement and entertainment industry. All kinds of positions within these areas can be found in commercial amusements parks, live theater or film productions, concerts and sporting events, and entertainment venues.

In addition to the people working in the categories described above, the leisure-oriented fields support a number of other occupations. These include people involved in the construction of facilities and areas; commercial establishments, such as stores, shops, and service stations located at or near major parks and resorts; and industries involved in the production of a great variety of recreation equipment—athletic gear, boats and motors, and fishing and hunting equipment. There are numerous other occupations that depend either completely or partly upon people's leisure time pursuits. It is apparent that if leisure time were suddenly eliminated, a major portion of the economy would suffer significant damage, and a very large number of people in a variety of occupations would become unemployed.

The world is on the cusp of new dimensions in travel and tourism. A short time ago the first tourist excursion was taken to the Antarctic, an area where only exploration parties had gone previously. In the future, tourist excursions under the sea and into outer space are certainly promising possibilities.

Occupations to Meet Society's Demands

The variety of leisure time activities is continually increasing as the number of people devoting their careers to leisure time occupations is on the rise. Leisure time occupations refer to various jobs that people engage in to provide opportunities for other people during leisure hours. These leisure time occupations are numerous and diverse.

The following list of titles or positions is but a sample of today's recreation and leisure service careers. Because of ever-evolving trends, we can't be certain what the future will produce; but we do know that the possibilities for recreation careers are increasing.

Airline staff
Amusement park director

Aquatics program director
Aquatics specialist
Armed forces recreation leader
Camp counselor
Camp director
Campground attendant
Carnival game operator
Casino manager
Church recreation director
College professor, leisure studies
Commercial game center director
Community center director
Community development specialist
Community education worker
Concert promoter
Concessionaire
Condominium social director
Convention and visitors bureau administrator
Corporate recreation specialist
Cruise ship activity director
Dance instructor
Environmental interpreter
Facility designer
Facility operator
Fisheries conservationist
Fitness specialist
Forester
Golf pro
High-rise recreation facilitator
Industrial recreation specialist

Leisure counselor
Leisure education specialist
Municipal recreation leader
Museum guide
Naturalist
Outdoor recreation manager
Outdoor and waterway guide
Outfitter
Park ranger
Park superintendent
Performing arts venue director
Playground leader
Prison recreation specialist
Professional sports administrator
Recreation facility manager
Recreation therapist
Resort manager
River guide
Rock climbing instructor
Senior citizen programmer
Ski instructor
Special populations programmer
Tennis pro
Theme park recreation coordinator or cast
Therapeutic recreation specialist
Tour guide
Travel planner
University activities center director
Volunteer agency supervisor
Wilderness trip guide

Wildlife biologist
Wildlife conservationist
Wildlife game protector
Youth agency recreator
Youth sports coach
Youth sports director
Zoological and botanical garden director

Some of these occupations are naturals for people who are highly skilled athletes or entertainers, especially if they have reputations that will attract clientele. Such persons might become golf pros, tennis or ski instructors, or summer theater directors. The curriculum that these people pursue in college is sometimes of little relevance—reputation, personality, and expertise are more important in attracting a clientele. However, for most recreation leadership roles, the best avenue is through a college program in some aspect of recreation and park management; one that prepares a person to assume a professional position and to advance as the opportunities come along. It is for these people that experience is often the key.

3

Diversity Within Recreation Careers

The calling of a leisure professional is one of ultimate dedication. For, not only are they investing time to increase the quality of life for other people, they are investing that energy which visualizes their innermost passion.

—Anonymous

As a profession, parks and recreation possesses the amazing characteristic to relate to obscure and even never-before-contemplated positions in the workforce. It is a career where people can ask what it is they love to do in their spare time, get an education related to that industry, and actively engage in their passion.

Someone who loves to canoe could own or manage an expedition company that takes people to paddle remote rivers. A meeting planner could become the social manager of a governmental official. A sports enthusiast could become the marketing associate for a professional team and help facilitate intermission activities to entertain spectators. Someone who loves to communicate, both written and verbally, could become a travel reporter or a promotions manager.

Types of Positions

The list of opportunities and possibilities is virtually endless. Any facet of recreation, whether as a supplier of equipment, a manager of a company, or an employee of a program, can be found in the field of parks and recreation. Here are some positions available in the parks, recreation, tourism, and leisure profession.

Professorship

According to the National Recreation and Parks Association, 809 faculty personnel were employed to prepare 2,070 graduates of college recreation curricula in 1967. Almost half of these teachers taught a portion of their load in other departments, or they taught only part-time at the college while engaging in other professional work. Generally speaking, the number of faculty members increases approximately in proportion to the number of graduates; in 2002 there were approximately thirteen thousand college and university faculty members involved in recreation and park curricula on either a full-time or part-time basis.

To qualify for a college teaching position, two or more years of highly successful professional experience are required along with at least a master's degree. Today a person holding a doctoral degree has a distinct advantage in the competition for college faculty positions. For more information regarding recreational educators, visit the Society of Park and Recreation Educators, a division of NRPA, at www.nrpa.org/content/default.aspx?documentid=531.

Therapeutic Recreation (TR)

Numerous hospitals, schools, and nursing and residential facilities have recreation programs in physical medicine, rehabilitation, pediatrics, psychiatry, and long-term care. The goal of these programs is to improve patient functioning skills through leisure activities. Such programs are based on a holistic approach; TR incorporates treatment, education, and inclusion by means of direct services provided to the consumer.

Smaller facilities often have only one recreation specialist on the staff, while some of the larger hospitals have several therapists, with one of them serving as the coordinator or supervisor of the program. Many are private for-profit, private nonprofit, or owned by the government, such as veterans hospitals. In governmental agencies, the employment conditions of TR specialists are defined by civil service specifications. Contact your state civil service office or the office in charge of the TR program at a particular hospital for employment opportunities in this area.

Those seeking therapeutic recreation positions must complete a specialized program in this field at a four-year college or university. A few positions are available for people who have completed an associate or two-year college program. This type of position is called a TR assistant. Most positions require a Certified Therapeutic Recreation Specialist (CTRS) credential from the National Council of Therapeutic Recreation Certification. For those who want additional training beyond a bachelor's degree, several institutions offer preparation at the master's degree level.

Therapeutic recreation used to be one of the fastest-growing areas of professional recreation. There is a limitation on the number of professionals that can be accommodated in this field because of the restricted population. However, more recently, decreased funding has affected the structure of government-run facilities. TR positions are sometimes the first to be eliminated. But different locations are appearing in the private sector, and consulting firms are employing many TR professionals.

TR professionals are utilized in several specialized areas, including gerontology, community development, disability management, substance abuse, physical rehabilitation, psychiatry, or pediatrics. Hospitals focus on treating patients. It is a problem-oriented clinical setting that incorporates assessment, treatment plans, and fun activities to serve the consumer. Residential settings look to teach—or reteach—skills that were lost due to a disability and work to foster inclusion. More information can be found by visiting the American Therapeutic Recreation Association at www.atra-tr.org.

Industrial/Corporate Recreation

Certain companies provide a recreation program for employees and their families as part of the employee benefits. Sometimes the employees' association or club sponsors the program. Industrial recreation agencies often own such specialized facilities as a private park, a golf course, or a hunting club. Such programs involve a variety of leagues and tournaments designed to furnish participation opportunities to employees in interesting and developmental activities. The exact responsibilities and working conditions of corporate recreation leaders vary from each other considerably, because each company is independent and different from any other. Further, the norms for professional qualifications and working conditions are less defined in this area of recreation than in most others. Anyone interested in entering this type of position should contact the Employee Services Management Association, formally the National Industrial Recreation Association, via its website at www.esmassn.org.

Armed Forces Recreation—Morale, Welfare, and Recreation (MWR)

Ever since World War II, the armed forces have been committed to providing ample recreational opportunities for military personnel and their dependents. The recreation leadership positions are filled by a combination of military personnel and civil service employees. Most positions are within the United States, but there are some opportunities at U.S. military stations in foreign countries.

A person entering this field would normally receive a low civil service rating; however, higher ratings are possible for people who have had extensive professional experience. For those interested in this form of employment, the best source of specific information is the nearest Civil Service Commission office or the Division of Special Services, which is found within each military branch in Washington, DC. Additional insight may be gained by looking at each branch of the military's MWR website. For example, the U.S. Army is at www.armymwr.com.

Private Clubs

Recreation leadership positions in private clubs come in a variety of forms. For example, the same club might employ a golf professional primarily as a teacher, an aquatics specialist to oversee the swimming program, and a clubhouse manager to oversee a variety of activities for the clubhouse. Other kinds of private clubs providing employment opportunities are tennis clubs, swim clubs, gun clubs, and health clubs (or health spas).

Success in most of these positions depends on a high level of skill in the particular activity involved, along with an appealing personality that will attract and hold clientele. For example, a golf or tennis pro must have a reputation as a performer, which will give him or her entry into a professional position. This will attract people to take lessons, which, in turn, will perpetuate the pro's professional image. Of course, success over a period of time will depend on how effectively the expert performs all aspects of the duties in that position. Visit the National Club Association at www.natlclub.org for more information.

Commercial Recreation

As in any business, commercial recreation is based upon a free enterprise system in which the individual, or company, prepares and distributes services and products in an effort to make a profit. This fact of business life (operating at a profit) forces the successful operator to remain sensitive and responsive to the public being served.

Job opportunities in commercial recreation are quite varied and historically have been relatively sparse. However, it is becoming more apparent that the unprecedented increase of Americans' recreational needs cannot be met solely by the local, state, and federal government agencies. The result is increased opportunities in commercial recreation.

Jobs in this field include such positions as owners, directors, supervisors, managers, and employees. They are found at places like boys' or girls' camps; wilderness tour or expedition organizations; recreation travel agencies; bowling and banquet facilities; amusement parks; outdoor outfitters; consulting firms for the planning of recreation areas, facilities, and programs; commercial waterfront or ski resorts; aquatics centers; skating rinks; professional sports; cruise ships, commercial venues; convention and visitors bureaus; meeting planning/special event coordinating firms; and casinos.

The success of commercial recreation enterprises and the personnel involved with them ranges from very poor to highly successful, just as in other kinds of businesses. Those going into commercial recreation need to be somewhat cautious and plan very carefully with respect to investment as compared to potential return. In addition, certain characteristics and abilities are vital to a successful entrepreneur. He or she must be able to meet the public effectively, have some ability as a personnel and financial manager, possess ingenuity and creativity, and have the ability for self-promotion. Carefully selected courses in business management and business procedures should be a part of any interested person's preparation.

Commercial recreation agencies that qualify can obtain federal financial assistance (low-interest loans) and planning assistance through the Small Business Administration. Also, certain states have assistance programs available to recreation and tourism enterprises. To take a closer look at commercial and for-profit opportunities, visit the Resort and Commercial Recreation Association website at www.r-c-r-a.org.

Tourism

The total travel industry is much broader than just its recreational aspects. But travel for pleasure is a significant part of the industry and, therefore, should be identified as a field of recreational employment opportunity. It is interesting that in forty-six of the fifty states, tourism ranks as one of the top three industries. This would seem to imply a massive number of job opportunities, but one should not be overly optimistic about this because most tourists travel by private automobile and make their own travel arrangements.

In spite of that, about 30 percent of the tourist travel occurs on airlines, buses, and trains, and a good portion of this involves organized tours. These tours may be sponsored and organized by nonprofit groups such as schools and religious, political, cultural, civic, professional, and community organizations.

Those employed in the tourist industry are involved mainly in arranging transportation, food and lodging, and entertainment. Anyone interested in tourism job opportunities needs to be interested in and prepared for promotional work, business management, personnel management, and public relations. The state office of tourism (every state has one) would be a good place to obtain specific information about tourism statistics and trends. For more information on development and careers in tourism, visit the website for the National Tourism Foundation at www.ntfonline.org.

Outdoor/Environmental Recreation and Resource Management

Approximately 699 million acres within the United States are designated for parks, recreation, wildlife refuges, and public institutions and facilities. The management, effective utilization, and preservation of this land with its complex soil, plant, and animal systems combined with people's desire for recreation and beauty opens up a variety of important career opportunities.

Outdoor recreation is based on facilitating hands-on recreation in nature. Some of the more familiar positions are interpreters, who use communication activities to improve understanding of sites like parks, zoos, museums, nature centers, historic sites, and aquariums; camp administrators, who work to facilitate programs in day or residential camps that offer participants life experiences; and park rangers, whose duties are much like interpreters, with an emphasis on enforcement of park law. However, it is important to note that there are many other options beyond these. There has been a major growth in adventure recreation, which has opened up vast opportunities for playground safety specialists, adventure trip leaders and expedition guides, and challenge course facilitators.

Positions in the natural resource management field include those for foresters to manage, develop, and protect wildlands and their resources; forestry aids and technicians to assist the forester with timber sales, supervise recreation area use, and be involved with public education, fire prevention, and research activities; range managers to develop, protect, and plan for the use of the one billion acres of rangeland in the United States, including recreation, grazing, timber, and watersheds; soil conservationists to plan, apply, and maintain programs for soil and water conservation, utilization, and treatment; wildlife conservationists to manipulate our soil, water, plants, and animals so as to produce the desired number of animals based on the best interests of humanity; and fishery conservationists to manage our commercial and sports fisheries, which supply and promote more than six hundred million recreation days per year in this country.

Those individuals interested in resource management are encouraged to take courses such as natural resource management, wildlife management, environmental interpretations, and outdoor systems management. Working summers out in the field while you are an undergraduate or getting internship experience before seeking a job would be very desirable.

If you are interested in interpretation, check out the National Association for Interpretation website at www.interpnet.com. Information on camp administration can be found at the American Camp Association website at www.acacamps.org. The Park Law Enforcement Association can provide insight into careers in this area; just visit its website at www.parkranger.com. Adventure programming information can be found at the American Association for Leisure and Recreation website at www.aahperd.org/aalr, the Association for Experimental Education at www.aee.org, and Project Adventure at www.pa.org.

For more information regarding resource management, there are several government organizations that you can contact: the National Resources Conservation Service at www.nrcs.usda.gov, the regional office of the U.S. Forest Service at www.fs.fed.us, the National Park Service at www.nps.gov, the Fish and Wildlife Service at www.fws.gov, the Bureau of Land Management at www.blm.gov, or other appropriate agencies.

Outdoor Education

This occupational field is closely related to outdoor recreation; however, it is separate in the sense that outdoor education in the schools is a branch of education requiring a teaching certificate. Those interested in this field ordinarily would qualify by pursuing a program in outdoor education, which would typically be offered through the College of Education. Upon completion, the person would seek employment with a school district as an outdoor education specialist.

There are some less formal approaches to outdoor education that offer a limited number of opportunities. For example, a few cities and some federal agencies manage outdoor education or interpretative centers where employees are specialists in outdoor education.

However, these employees are not necessarily certified to teach in a school system.

For anyone interested in outdoor education, a good source of specific information is the Outdoor Education Research and Evaluation Center. The website is www.wilderdom.com.

Choosing a Generalized or Specialized Position

As indicated, there are certain positions in this field that require a high degree of specialization, whereas other positions require more generalized preparation. Whether you should prepare to be a specialist or a generalist depends on the nature of the position to which you aspire. Obviously, if you want to be a golf or tennis professional or teach fitness or do leisure counseling, you must be a specialist of the highest order and generalized preparation is only of supplementary value.

Conversely, if you are preparing to be a recreation supervisor or eventually the director of a program, generalized preparation covering a broad scope of the field would give you a stronger base for achieving your aspirations. The earlier in your professional preparation you can decide what you want to accomplish in your profession, and on what time schedule, the better prepared you will be to determine the degree of specialization or generalization you should pursue. There are places in this field for both generalists and specialists, but these two kinds of employment require quite different preparation and experience.

Employment Options in the Field

Once you've chosen a career area, you should decide what role you'd like to have within it. Usually, roles are not exclusive. For example, administrative, supervisory, directorship, and leadership may have duty and role characteristics that overlap. It is important to determine which best fits your personality, abilities, and desires.

Administration

These positions involve planning, organizing, and administering a recreation and/or park program to meet the needs and interests of those being served. The title might be manager, director, superintendent, or executive. Most administrators are responsible for both recreation programming and park management; however, sometimes these two major responsibilities are placed under separate administrators. Typically, the responsibilities of the administrator include the following:

- Oversee work of the department in accordance with prescribed policies and basic procedures that usually are established by a governing board or commission.
- Be an active component of the board or commission in planning future direction.
- Recruit, select, assign, supervise, and evaluate the departmental staff.
- Oversee the acquisition, planning, construction, improvement, and maintenance of areas and facilities.
- Prepare the annual budget proposal, administer the budget, and account for all revenues and expenditures.
- Give leadership to the public relations efforts of the department.
- Provide administrative guidance to supervisors and center directors to be sure their phases of the program are managed effectively.

- Arrange in-service training to improve the performance of staff members.
- Instigate, support, and evaluate research studies relating to the departmental operation.
- Motivate and inspire departmental personnel.

The required training of an administrator varies considerably with the size and complexity of the tasks and the department. It usually includes graduation from a recognized college or university with at least a bachelor's degree in recreation administration, park management, or some closely related field, plus successful experience over a period of several years. A graduate degree is often helpful, and it is sometimes required. Substantial evidence of a sound philosophy and superior management ability outweigh most other considerations.

Supervisory

Representing a secondary level of administration, supervisors are responsible for all of the activities and/or facilities within a specific geographic area (general supervisor) or for a specialized area of the program (special supervisor). A supervisor of a district would be responsible for the administration of all or specified portions of the recreation program and facilities in the designated geographic area.

The responsibilities would be very similar to those of the department administrator, except the supervisor's responsibilities would pertain only to a portion of the community. A special supervisor would be responsible for a specialized phase of the program, such as athletics, aquatics, or social activities. Usually a department would not have both general (geographic) supervisors and special (activity) supervisors, but would have one or the other. However, in some large departments there are supervisors of both kinds.

Normally the qualifications for supervisors include a bachelor's degree in recreation or a closely related field, along with a specified period of experience.

Directors of Centers and Special Facilities

A community or neighborhood center is a multipurpose recreation complex that needs to be under the leadership of an administrator who is effective in promotion, programming, and working with people, particularly the residents and individuals in the vicinity of the center. The director is in charge of the staff and the facility and has the responsibility of utilizing these effectively to accomplish the purposes of the center. Ordinarily, the director is responsible to an area supervisor or to the department administrator.

Another kind of director is the one placed in charge of a special facility or a facility more singular in purpose than a neighborhood center, such as a botanic garden, a zoo, a waterfront area, a museum, or a cultural center. A person holding one of these positions is usually a specialist in the particular area of interest for which the center is designed. Here again, the director would be responsible for using the staff, facilities, and other resources as effectively as possible to accomplish the purposes of the special center.

Direct Leadership

Direct leaders are those who furnish face-to-face leadership to people. Direct leaders have such responsibilities as organizing and directing athletic contests, directing aquatics programs, teaching dance, preparing concerts and recitals, promoting and directing dramatics productions, and leading children in playground activities.

For full-time direct leadership positions, a college degree in recreation or a related field is generally required. Two years of college study gives sufficient preparation for certain positions, while a degree from a four-year college or university is usually required for most upper-level management positions. College students who have the necessary qualifications or teachers who enjoy this kind of summer employment often fill part-time or summer jobs.

4

THE FORCES OF CHANGE
AFFECTING EMPLOYMENT

If it isn't broke, break it!

—Edward Mahoney

IN RECENT DECADES, it seems that as soon as people get used to the latest change, it is replaced by yet another. Many of these changes relate to leisure and create a need for flexible professionals. This new breed of professionals needs to have adequate preparation and leadership in leisure time activities. Changes in the field and probable future developments are discussed in this chapter.

Work and Leisure

Work and leisure are the two sides of our shields. The one side—work—enables us to live while the other side makes living more meaningful.

The average workweek in America in 1850 was almost seventy hours; in 1900 it was fifty-five hours; and by 1950 it had been reduced to about forty hours. Some occupational groups are now on workweeks of fewer than forty hours. Economic and labor specialists predict that in the near future, Americans will average only thirty-six hours of work per week.

While the hours spent working become shorter, weekends are fuller. Vacation periods become longer. People are retiring at an earlier age. When these trends are analyzed, it is apparent that Americans today spend significantly more time at leisure than ever before.

The total amount of leisure tells only part of the story; distribution of time and the length of its increments are other important factors. Daily leisure usually comes in segments of one to several hours following a day of labor. Weekly leisure is defined in terms of weekends, many of which will be three days in the future. Annual vacation time represents a longer period that the worker has earned after a year of labor.

The average American now lives to an age of about seventy-nine, with women living an average of about seven years longer than men. Because of the increased life expectancy, after retirement, individuals may have two to three decades that consists of, predominantly, discretionary time.

Time, whether it is involved with work or leisure, cannot be stored or saved or consumed at a rate faster than it is produced. Rich people have neither more nor less time than poor people. Like all other forms of time, leisure must be consumed either by doing something or by doing nothing.

Some people become slaves of their own possessions instead of creative users of their leisure. Many people know a neighbor or friend whose material goods intended for leisure (boats, campers, snowmobiles, skiing equipment, vacation homes) are so extensive that their lives are dominated by trying to pay for them. For some, the pleasure appears to be in the possession of such items and not in the joy of participation.

It is obvious that even with an abundance of leisure and with the promise of more to come, each person must still be highly selective about how he or she uses leisure time. Leisure can be a great blessing, but to some it may become a curse due to boredom, participation in poorly selected activities, or overindulgence of one kind or another.

Changing Philosophy

Leisure and recreation traditionally have been viewed with suspicion, while work has been held as one of the highest values of American life. Moreover, work traditionally has been associated with more than material accomplishments; it has been a source of social and moral recognition.

Even though contemporary concepts do not, and should not, minimize the values of work, they do express greater appreciation for leisure and participation in wholesome recreational pursuits. People today realize that wholesome recreation contributes to one's personality and adds to life a spirit of adventure, creativity, and enrichment.

The fundamental truth that recreation is essential to the cultural, moral, and spiritual well-being of people in a society has been reaffirmed. The challenge to use leisure time effectively and constructively demands the full development of local, state, and national resources; it also requires a sufficient amount of high-quality, dedicated leadership.

Automation

Some people argue that at worst, automation simply changes people's occupations; at best, it creates additional jobs. The industrial leaders and the United States Department of Labor indicate that several thousand jobs per week are eliminated in the United States as a result of automation.

This condition is partly counterbalanced by maintaining the workforce numbers but reducing the hours each person spends on the job. This is evidenced by the fact that more than seven hundred companies in the United States have all, or most, of their workers on a four-day workweek, and at least one thousand other companies are contemplating such a shift. In 1973 the nation's largest employer, the federal government, began to experiment with the four-day workweek, as did the municipalities of Atlanta, Long Beach, and Phoenix. A dozen companies, including Metropolitan Life Insurance, have gone even further, assigning some of their workers to a three-day week on an experimental basis.

Some experts believe that automation has only begun its replacement of people; they believe that within the next two decades we shall see an unprecedented rise in unemployment among the skilled and middle management groups, as well as the uneducated. They predict a society where a smaller percentage of the population will provide the basic necessities for all. If these predictions are realized, then truly one of the greatest needs in America will be a large number of well-prepared people in the various leisure time occupations. The provision of enriching and uplifting leisure time activities will become fundamental to a strong society and high-quality living.

Population

Both the number and the distribution of people influence the amount and kinds of opportunities and leadership that are needed. It is interesting that worldwide approximately 220 babies are born each minute while about 140 people die. In other words, if your heart rate is normal (seventy-two beats per minute), about three people are added while two people die with each beat of your heart. At this rate the world's population increases each week by about .73 million.

The population of the United States almost doubled from 1900 to 1950, an increase from 85 million to 151 million. Then, during the next forty years (1950 to 1990), it increased another 89 million, bringing the total to 240 million. Currently the United States is growing at a rate of about 3 million people per year. In percentage, the increase is lower than it has ever been, but in numbers the rate is still very dramatic.

Another interesting characteristic of population is age distribution. A male child born in 1900 could expect to live forty-six years, whereas one born in 2000 had a life expectancy of seventy-seven years. For females, the gain has been even greater, from forty-eight years in 1900 to eighty years in 2000. What will life expectancy increase to in the years to come?

In 1940, 25 percent of the population was fifteen and under; by 2000 this figure had increased to 28.6 percent. In 1940, 10 percent of the population was age sixty or more; by 2000 that percentage had reached 16.2 percent. The proportion of both young and old members of the population (nonworking ages) is increasing steadily.

Of course, the population in the United States does not live in isolation from the rest of the world. Therefore, population trends worldwide are important to know.

Most of the world's human population lives in underdeveloped countries or in countries where the natural resources are nearly depleted. This factor—of large, poverty-stricken populations—contributes to social unrest and political instability. It smothers efforts to develop better lives by the millions of people who are ill-fed, ill-clothed, ill-housed, poorly educated, and who lack the basic requirements of an enriched life.

Currently, North America and Western Europe have about 12 percent of the world's population and 64 percent of the income as measured in goods and services produced. Asia has nearly 57 percent of the population and 14 percent of the income. The deprived and underprivileged portion of the world's population is increasing more rapidly than the affluent portion.

It has been calculated that if the present rate of population growth had existed since the beginning of the Christian era, we would now have an average of one square yard of earth for each living person. That would hardly be enough for breathing room, much less mountain climbing, skiing, and long golf drives. Further, it has been calculated that if the present rate of increase continues, the earth's resources will simply not be able to sustain the population.

Technology

Visualize the amount of human energy that would be needed to propel an automobile sixty miles per hour for just one mile. Further, visualize the human effort that it would take to generate and deliver the electricity for running our refrigerators, disposals, electric lights, and heating or air-conditioning units over a twenty-four-hour period. Think of the thousands of hours that would be spent making calculations that can be accomplished on a computer in just thirty seconds. Even more impressive is the equivalent energy spent on a four-engine jetliner streaking through space at six hundred miles per hour or a one-hundred-car freight train traveling at fifty miles per hour.

These technological time- and energy-saving items are largely responsible for the increased leisure that is available Other technical devices also influence how we use our leisure in recreational pursuits. For example, powerboating and waterskiing are newfound pleasures that depend directly upon technology. The same is true for downhill skiing, underwater motorized exploration, driving for pleasure, and recreation involving aircraft and off-the-road vehicles. The technological influence on many other recreational pursuits, though substantial, is less direct. For example, the availability of electricity, better modes of travel and transportation, and more advanced objects enhance our experiences with, say, sports equipment and hunting and fishing gear.

Technology experts predict that we shall make more technological progress in the next twenty years than was made in any equivalent period of the past. A generation of computers is coming along fast without waiting for the rest of us to deal with the wholesale changes that will result. The computers of the future will be fast enough to do a decade of work during a lunch hour, and their impact will be felt not only by blue-collar workers but by skillful technicians and management personnel as well. American scientists see real possibilities for developing electric automobiles, nonpetroleum aircraft fuel, abundant solar energy units for heating, and a host of other new time-saving and energy-saving devices. Also, significant strides will continue toward improved household implements, making household management less time consuming.

A technologist is truly a significant contributor to the leisure lifestyle, both on and off the job. In the future, technological advances will give us significantly more time and more recreational alternatives to choose from. As a result, technology will contribute to leisure time job opportunities and will also help influence the nature of these jobs.

Mobility

Possibly the most distinctive feature of life in America is its mobility. Whether we travel by land, air, or sea for long or short distances, comfortable and rapid transportation is available. The most common mode, by far, is the automobile, followed respectively by air, train, and boat travel. At the present time the entire U.S. population could be seated comfortably in their privately owned cars, and the average would be only about 2.5 persons per car.

Even though the automobile is still our primary means of travel, other transportation modes have become increasingly important. In 1940 there were 2.5 million air passengers reported. This number reached a staggering 650 million in 2004, according to *USA Today*. The jetliner, which can reduce a land trip of sixteen hours to five hours by air, has revolutionized transportation. It has made virtually all parts of the nation accessible within a day's travel. The world's remarkable mobility will afford people in large numbers the opportunity to spend more of their increased leisure time in areas of their choice, and this will have significant effects on people's recreational patterns.

Education

There has been an awakening of average citizens to the fact that a high level of education is essential if they are to live effectively in our complex society. As a result, not only has the total number of students greatly increased, so has the average level of education. In 1910 only 63 percent of school-age children (five to eighteen years) were enrolled in school. By 1930 this had risen to 72 percent, and it is presently around 74 percent.

A greater number of students are going to college. College enrollments increased from 2.5 million in 1950 to 3.2 million in 1960 and to 6 million in 1970. The present college enrollment exceeds 9 million. The great move toward a college education is further demonstrated by the fact that in the early 1950s only 27 percent of college-age students were enrolled in college; this number has now reached about 34 percent.

This increased attention to education has two startling effects on planning for recreation. First, education is the key to higher personal income. Higher income influences what people do for recreation and where they go to do it. Second, as people further their education, they tend to broaden their horizon of interests, appreciations, and skills in recreation pursuits. Therefore, educated people tend to have not only more varied recreational interests but also more means with which to pursue them.

Income

Today's consumers are more than two-and-one-half times better off than the consumers in the mid-1930s, and 18 percent better off than consumers in the best economic years during World War II.

American consumers today have more purchasing power than ever before.

Based on the recent past, it is safe to assume that in the future, people will spend more money on hobbies, sports, adventure, and other types of recreation that provide increased satisfaction. Many will own two homes, one of which will be in a resort area. Two-car families will become three-car families, and the cars will be used more for pleasure than necessity. Boats, camping equipment, athletic gear, hunting and fishing supplies, ski equipment, hobby supplies, and other recreational goods and services will be purchased in ever-increasing amounts. In the coming years, leisure activities will capture an even greater amount of the individual's income and will contribute increasingly to the nation's economy.

Environmental Crisis

The quality of the environment will continue to be a major issue. The sight of natural beauty, the breathing of clean air, and the availability of clear, pure water are becoming rare to many Americans because the environment in many areas has become degraded and polluted. It is difficult, if not impossible, for people to have satisfying and enriching outdoor experiences under such conditions. One of the important contributions of people in leisure time occupations is their real concern for the environment and their leadership in improving conditions.

Overcrowded Facilities

In populated areas, overcrowded parks, playgrounds, and swimming pools are not uncommon, and these conditions will become even more common in the absence of adequate leadership. Often in areas where recreation facilities are inadequate, people seem willing to spend their money on nonproductive expenditures such as overusing their automobiles, purchasing unnecessary gadgets, and drinking, smoking, and overeating. As part of the educational process as it relates to leisure time, people need to learn that adequate facilities for enriching and developmental activities are far more important than some of the amusement activities on which people presently squander money. This educational process involves developing a sound set of values relating to life in general and to leisure time activities in particular.

Violence and Social Unrest

Demonstrations of unrest and violence and the apparent underlying causes are matters that should be of concern to all responsible citizens and particularly to those involved in planning leisure time activities. Some of these problems can be avoided, and many of them can be at least partially solved by providing an adequate amount of satisfying leisure time opportunities. Certainly leisure programs do not offer the total solution to such problems, but those in leisure occupations can make a significant contribution toward some constructive solutions.

5

PERSONAL INVESTMENT AND PROFESSIONAL CHARACTERISTICS

Tell me and I forget, teach me and I remember, involve me and I learn.

—Benjamin Franklin

AS EACH YEAR passes, it brings a new perspective and liberation from the past. Society finds itself in an environment of new opportunity for personal enrichment. People are now more free to think, feel, and exercise impulses without worrying about the bare essentials of life. Our age does not experience the survival needs that our forefathers did. To take advantage of this circumstance, the average American must be taught how to use leisure time to its fullest potential.

Leaders are needed to teach people this valuable knowledge and direct them in leisure pursuits. In addition to the task of working directly with people, professionals are needed to help on a larger scale. These skillful individuals will communicate purposes and appreciations, encourage the installation of adequate recreation facilities, and accept the combination of these two types of professionals that allows large numbers of people to achieve enrichment in their lives.

Personal Requirements

While highly specialized jobs require their own particular individual characteristics, there are some personal traits that are essential for leadership positions in the recreational field. Any person who contemplates entering this field should determine if his or her personality and the characteristics of the profession that follow below are compatible:

- Ability to work effectively with a public consisting of various ages and backgrounds.
- Sensitivity to the kinds of leisure time opportunities people need to round out their lives and achieve fulfillment.
- A sound sense of values on which accurate, appropriate decisions and leadership efforts will be based.
- A range of skills, interests, and appreciations that can be transformed into offerings to which people can, and will, devote their leisure time.
- A sincere interest in public service and the positive development of individuals and society.
- The specific knowledge and skills necessary for the field. For example, an administrator of a recreation program must be able to lobby effectively for a mileage increase. A designer of recreation facilities must be able to determine the necessary number and placement of trash receptacles. A recreation

coordinator must be able to determine age-appropriate cognitive and motor-skill activities.

- A personable individual whom members of the public will respect and look toward for leadership.
- A cooperative attitude and a dedication to creating partnerships among individuals and agencies involved in leisure time pursuits.
- Common sense, which will help in understanding and dealing with people in various situations.
- The ability to enjoy life and to motivate others to do the same.

Park and recreation professionals must continue their progress toward overcoming their long-time public image as playground babysitters or public groundskeepers. Their responsibilities are too great for this image to continue. It's important to concentrate on making people aware of the benefits of the field. At the same time they must continue to enhance their image by constant development of their qualifications as executives, innovators, planners, teachers, supervisors, and leaders of broad and complex leisure-oriented programs of real quality and meaning.

Park and recreation professionals must be competent in working with natural and man-made areas supervised by government and nongovernment agencies to make the best use of their aesthetic, functional, and economic potential. These professionals must always be aware that the resources are for the optimum use of people.

Professional Goals

One of the distinct characteristics of a profession is a broad commitment by its members to certain fundamental values or objectives. The members of a profession are not expected to think alike at all times, but they are obligated to agree upon central purposes. Such an agreement is essential to providing unity and ensuring the survival of the profession.

Almost twenty-five hundred years ago, Socrates emphasized the importance of goals when he said, "If a man does not know to what port he is sailing, no wind is favorable." The challenge of having clear direction has real pertinence to the individual leader because his or her worth will be no greater than the values sought. Further, leaders with unsound values tend not only to be worthless but also have the potential for being dangerous to society.

Fortunately, in 1964 the American Association for Health, Physical Education, and Recreation established the Commission on Goals for American Recreation. The commission, consisting of outstanding leaders from throughout the nation, prepared statements that have had significant impact. Any person considering the recreation profession ought to become familiar with these goals, in addition to giving serious thought to what he or she wants to achieve individually. Following are condensed descriptions of the goals established by the commission.

Personal Fulfillment

Since the American democratic ideal is rooted in a conviction of superior importance to the individual, it follows that the individual's welfare and personal development should be a goal of public and private programs that are geared toward service. In accord with this concept, the paramount purpose of recreational activities is to enrich the lives of people by contributing to their fulfillment as individuals, while at the same time helping them fit more comfortably into the social structure.

It is natural for people to be motivated by the basic needs of adequacy and self-enrichment. Nobody wants to be a nobody. Individuals want to see themselves as accepted, able, and successful. The extent to which this need is met is a measure of personal fulfillment, while the lack of fulfillment contributes to frustration and often maladjustment.

One of the foremost challenges to people in the recreation profession is to provide experience through which an individual may enjoy success in the search for self-esteem. It is the task of a leader to assist participants in the development of skills and appreciations that enrich them and result in true satisfaction.

Democratic Human Relations

There are three important reasons why recreation involvement contributes to the qualities of a good citizen in a democracy.

1. A recreation agency in the United States is a social institution in a democratic nation. Therefore, the leaders are under obligation to seek social, moral, and ethical values that will preserve and strengthen the democracy.

2. Exclusive emphasis on goals focused primarily on the individual may result in the creation of selfishness and noncooperation. Recreation agencies, along with other institutions in society, have the responsibility to help develop those characteristics of good citizenship that are essential in a democracy. Responsibility, respect, service to others, problem solving, and developing positive relationships are traits that are enforced through leisure activities.

3. Whether they understand or desire it, recreation leaders are inescapably involved in the conduct of activities whose outcomes go far beyond fun, relaxation, and immediate fulfillment. Experi-

ence in recreation, like other experiences in life, influence one's personality in many respects.

Leisure Skills and Interests

It is no coincidence that the words *skills* and *interests* appear together often. Skill is the foundation upon which interest is built, and interest leads to further development of skill. In their leisure time, if opportunities are available, people do what they like to do and often like to do what they do well. A high degree of skill in a wholesome activity is the best single guarantee of interest. Not many people, for example, are clamoring to demonstrate their ineptitude in tennis, golf, art, music, ballroom dancing, or swimming. There is plenty of evidence to support the claim that people repeat those experiences that are satisfying and avoid those that are not. Therefore, developing skills and interests in wholesome activities is fundamental to the well-rounded development of an individual and to the good life.

Several research studies support the claim that people use their leisure time in the skills and interests developed early in life. There is also evidence that what people like at age twenty-five they like better with increased age, and what they dislike at age twenty-five they dislike more as age advances. Recreation leaders have a strong obligation to be teachers of interests and skills at a level of excellence to both youth and adults, cultivating in them a taste for beauty in art, music, dance, and literature; helping them to achieve excellence in sports and games; and offering a discovery into the beauty of nature while maintaining a highly livable environment.

Health and Fitness

In early history, most people had no choice between the sedentary and active life; the necessities of survival forced them to be active. However, modern men and women have choices, and urbanization and technology have reduced opportunities for vigorous exercise. Today, of the physical work done in the United States, 1 percent is by animals, 1 percent is by people, and 98 percent is by machines. Automation is the servant of the sedentary life.

Prior to our mass-motorized transportation system, people generally walked to most places. Today we ride automobiles with power brakes, power steering, power windows, and power seats. Even on the golf course, motorized carts have become a substitute for human energy. Elevators carry people upstairs and electric eyes open doors. An individual, on average, sits in front of the television for twenty-seven hours per week. Most engage in sport merely as spectators, and the most popular outdoor recreation is driving for pleasure. Several degenerative diseases and a general lack of efficiency have greatly accelerated with our modern sedentary living patterns.

In connection with fitness and health, the challenges and opportunities in the field of recreation are apparent. If our work does not supply us with the activity we need for good health and fitness, then this must be accomplished during leisure hours.

Another interesting aspect of active living is the contribution it can make toward mental health and emotional stability. Participation in pleasurable pursuits is important to the release of tension and mental stress.

Creative Expression and Aesthetic Appreciation

To give depth and richness to life, emphasis needs to be placed on creative experiences and aesthetics. Industrial and technological advances have created an emphasis on practicality, which has generally detracted from artistic and personal expression. There seems to be a lack of serenity in which creative thought and talent may be fostered. One of the important purposes of recreation is to stimulate and guide creativity that otherwise might never surface. Pursuits that relate to aesthetic values have great potential for giving zest to life, and the profession needs well-qualified leaders who are innovative and who have the ability to stimulate others and draw out of them their innate creativity.

Environment for Living in a Leisure Society

The environment in which each of us recreates, either alone or with others, has a great influence on the quality of the recreation experience. One of the tragedies of our time is the degradation and destruction of natural resources that heretofore sustained both body and soul. We have become too free in the use of tools and machines for converting natural products to utilitarian ends, serving only today's needs. This has contributed to an artificial and culturally sterile environment that does not serve the long-term needs of the people. In the future, we will have to guard with increased vigor against this destructive trend.

The recreational environment in cities and suburbs is equally important as the great outdoors, and the problem of maintaining it at a high level is even more difficult. About 79 percent of the American population now lives in urban and suburban areas, and the trend in both numbers and percentages is still rising. The U.S. Census Bureau predicts that in the near future, 80 percent of Americans will be urban dwellers. Only with expert planning and leadership will highly livable city environments be developed and maintained. Sustaining such environments will be one of the great challenges of the future, particularly for recreation planners and administrators.

6

Education in Recreation and Leisure

Our surroundings can enrich or impoverish our lives. Thus conserving and improving our environment can add immeasurably to private and public happiness.

—Hubert H. Humphrey

THE FIELD OF recreation has broadened immensely over the past decade. Today, jobs in the field run the spectrum and include those found in administrative, supervisory, and other leadership positions. Employment is found in public, private, and volunteer settings. Professionals in this field equip themselves with education and professional experiences.

Generally speaking, the professional in this field must be a promoter, a planner, an organizer, a teacher, and a motivator. If he or she is to serve a worthwhile purpose, his or her efforts must be based on a sound sense of values that will cause leadership to actually benefit people. No wonder those who work in this interesting field find it challenging, exciting, and rewarding.

A major goal among those in the park and recreation field is the development of a clear and favorable public image—an image of professional competency and dedicated service. In fact, in the past there has been a serious lack of public knowledge about the scope and opportunities in leisure time occupations, and particularly about the recreation profession. However, because of the increased demand of leisure time occupations in recent years, and because of the strong present trend in that direction, this lack of understanding is being overcome rapidly. There is an increased awareness in communities across the nation of the need for competent and well-prepared recreational leaders.

Early Career Development

Most leisure time occupations involve working effectively with people. Further, these occupations usually involve a knowledge and intense interest in a variety of activities. You can begin preparing for a leisure time career while still in high school. Communications, art, physical education, and vocational arts provide a valuable background. Other courses that furnish leadership experiences, improve your ability to speak effectively, and teach you how to understand people are also beneficial.

Participation in extracurricular activities is strongly recommended. Sports, dramatics, music, debate, editing of school publications, participation in hobby groups, and volunteering help to develop skills, special interests, and ability to work with others.

The U.S. Department of Education has designed a bold program of career education in which the various career fields that students in secondary schools ought to consider have been grouped into fifteen clusters. One of the clusters is identified as leisure careers.

Robert M. Worthington, associate commissioner of the U.S. Department of Education, made the following statement about leisure careers:

> Of the fifteen clusters forming this new design, the leisure careers are among the most promising. Americans seeking leisure time experiences will create millions of new jobs in the near future. Many of these jobs will be innovative and imaginative. Their environments will range from the natural wilderness to electronic playgrounds, and perhaps even more important, central to the leisure careers is personal interaction—a facet the majority of today's youth demand in a job.

This statement indicates a trend in leisure career employment.

The U.S. Department of Education Career Development Program, which encompasses four important phases, is one that can be initiated and designed by school administrators and teachers, or students can do it for themselves. The purpose of the career development approach is to help you determine more intelligently where your interests lie and what abilities you have.

• **Phase 1: Career Awareness.** This phase should start early in a student's education and does not necessarily have an ending point. It includes recognition of the personal and social significance of work, fosters an awareness of the many occupations that one might consider, and builds aspirations to be productive and to succeed.

• **Phase 2: Career Exploration.** This phase provides experiences related to the field that will assist students in evaluating their interests, abilities, values, and deeds with regard to occupational roles. It also makes basic subject matter more meaningful and relevant through focusing around a clearly developed theme.

• **Phase 3: Career Orientation.** The purpose of this phase is to provide in-depth training in one of the occupational clusters while still leaving open the option to move to a different occupational field. There is a focus of subject matter even more directly to a career development theme. This phase also should include guidance and counseling relative to preparing for a particular field.

• **Phase 4: Skill Development.** The purpose of this phase is to provide the student with specific intellectual and performance skills in a selected occupational cluster or specific occupational field to better prepare him or her for job entry and/or continuing education. Further, the purpose is to motivate the student to become committed to developing excellence both in him or herself and in the chosen occupational field.

This four-phase approach will make you more aware of the opportunities and requirements of any career field. For a basic awareness of the leisure career field, you need answers to these questions: What is leisure? What is the leisure career field? What are the opportunities for employment and advancement? What is the future occupational outlook in this field? What are the basic requirements for employment? What approach is best to prepare for a chosen occupational specialty?

Professional Preparation Programs

Recreation and park curricula currently exist within more than 200 two-year and approximately 700 four-year college campuses in North America. There has been a phenomenal increase in the number of curricula since the end of World War II, when there were approximately a dozen. By 1950 there were thirty-eight college curricula. In 1960 there were sixty-three. In 1970, 227 institutions reported curricula in this field, and in 1982 the number totaled 354. These numbers, according to *Peterson's Guide*, have continued to grow—to 897—and are expected to rise as recreation and leisure careers gain acceptance in the fact that practitioners require specialized knowledge, training, and abilities. The number of doctoral and master's degree programs has also increased over the past decade.

The curriculum is housed in a variety of divisions and departments including health, physical education, and recreation; education; forestry; natural resources; arts and sciences; and business, marketing, and public relations. It is important, too, to recognize that the college and university recreation departments are not the only programs involved in engaging potential professionals in this field. A portion of the employees in the leisure industries have degrees in liberal arts, physical education, forestry, sociology, business, landscape architecture, industrial arts, and the fine arts.

However, because the recreation and leisure industry desires professionals with specialized knowledge and training, employers prefer individuals who have degrees from an accredited institution. Accreditation is granted to a recreation department of a university, a college, or an agency when it meets or exceeds a level of educational quality. This is achieved through strict scrutiny by the professional organizations within the field responsible for setting the standards of the profession. The National Recreation and Park Association (NRPA) and the American Association for Leisure and Recreation (AALR) are responsible for developing these standards. Currently, there are one hundred accredited universities in North America.

Within the accredited curriculum, the institution must develop courses that educate students to meet or exceed competencies in core topics. The NRPA/AALR Council on Accreditation have determined that the organization of the university department is important; it should be based on faculty contributions and professional development, goals and philosophies of the department as a whole in contributing to student education and the profession, office and course administration, and resources available for instruction.

Another area of significance is the content of programs offered. Emphasis is placed on general requirements, which act as a foundation for a student's base of knowledge. Courses must involve concepts of strategic planning and evaluation of an agency; legal aspects manifested in risk management; legislative administration; event programming; practical experiences and internships; and agency administration, which involves budgeting, human resources, marketing, and volunteers.

Departments have to decide on the options they wish to offer to their students, and within each of those areas, they must express specific merit and contribution to development in the field. Those areas include leisure services management, natural resources recreation management, leisure/recreation program delivery, and therapeutic recreation.

Whether accredited or not, recreation and leisure curricula are found across the United States and Canada in the form of associate's, bachelor's, master's, and doctorate programs. Following is an overview of each degree program. A list of schools in the United States and Canada offering recreation and leisure-related curricula can be found in Appendix A.

Associate Degree Programs

Today approximately two hundred two-year colleges offer curricula in the recreation and park field. The rapid increase in two-year associate degree programs can be attributed to two major factors: expansion of the number of two-year colleges, and the demand for direct leaders and program technicians who need less than a four-year college degree. The role of two-year associate degree programs in recreation is to prepare students for face-to-face leadership positions or technician jobs. These programs prepare students for early entry into the field and/or transfer to four-year programs to continue education toward a bachelor's degree. The kinds of jobs available to people with associate degrees include director of playground activities, swimming pool manager or swimming instructor, leader of athletic activities, park ranger (in some areas), and park maintenance supervisor.

Bachelor's Degree Programs

Typically, in bachelor degree programs about 50 percent of the course work is in general education, including humanities, language arts, physical and social sciences, and English and writing skills. The remaining 50 percent is in a specialized field and related electives. In addition to course work in the specialty, a student majoring in recreation ordinarily has extensive on-the-job training under the combined supervision of a specialist in the field and a faculty supervisor. As stated earlier, nearly seven hundred colleges and universities in the United States offer bachelor's degrees in the recreation and park field.

Graduate Preparation

Often the administrators of the large and more complex recreation and park programs are required to hold master's degrees, and college teachers and research specialists almost always must earn at least a master's degree and, preferably, a doctorate. The areas that ordinarily receive emphasis at the graduate level include philosophy and principles related to recreation and leisure, administrative philosophy and procedures, research and evaluation techniques, advanced approaches to personal management, and public relations. Sometimes more specialized areas are pursued at the graduate levels, such as therapeutic recreation, management of outdoor recreation resources, or park administration. Currently there are 122 schools in the United States that offer master's degree programs and 20 that offer doctorate-level programs. Within Canada there are 10 universities that offer postbaccalaureate degrees.

Scholarships and Internships

The National Recreation and Park Association (NRPA) administers a national internship program that provides special advanced training for a number of college graduates showing outstanding potential for administrative careers in the field. Stipends varying from $8,000 to $10,000 per year are awarded by agencies selected to oversee these internships. The host agency also provides a broad-based and diversified experience designed to move the intern quickly into a responsible administrative position. These agencies are located throughout the country and are representative of all facets of the park, recreation, and conservation field. Information about how to apply may be obtained from the NRPA. Its website is www.nrpa.org.

The scholarship office of every college or university will furnish information upon request about scholarships offered by the particular institution. In some cases, the specific department where the recreation curriculum is administered has limited financial aid available for selected students.

7

Opportunities
for Employment

People pay for what they do. And even more for who they become.
They pay simply by the lives that they lead.

—James Baldwin

LEISURE CAREER OPPORTUNITIES within the broad spectrum of
parks, recreation, and conservation will involve critical issues ranging from inner cities to the wilderness of the great outdoors, and
from face-to-face interaction with people to the less personal, but
equally meaningful, elements of rivers and forests. In every instance,
regardless of the special interest area pursued, people will be the ultimate beneficiaries. The leaders and workers who give direction and
impetus to this vast effort will come from many walks of life, and
they will be involved in a variety of ways. The following discussion
will help you gain insight into present and future opportunities and
working conditions in the recreation and parks professions.

Changing Faces

Approximately 40 percent of the college students majoring in recreation and park curricula are women. Employment opportunities for women are expansive. A woman who is well qualified for this field will find plenty of opportunity for gainful employment if she is willing to locate herself in the areas where the opportunities exist.

In the past, employment of minorities in the field of recreation has been concentrated in large cities, but is it becoming more widespread. Federal agencies are bound by law to give equal opportunity to members of minority groups and to women. The same requirements for equal opportunities exist in state government. The recreation occupations reflect this trend toward equal employment opportunities for persons of commensurate abilities, and salaries for women and members of minority groups are also required by law to be the same as salaries for other employees in parallel positions.

In addition to planning programs and services for the population as a whole, substantial effort must be directed toward special population groups whose needs are related to economic inadequacies and/or environmental deficiencies. Very often the culturally, educationally, and economically disadvantaged are the same individuals who are recreationally disadvantaged. Therefore, to some degree, they lack opportunities for preparing themselves to become effective leaders in recreational programs. However, there are many individual exceptions to this. Further, some program administrators arrange workshops and clinics to help prospective disadvantaged employees meet any challenges.

Employment of individuals who are disadvantaged is especially relevant to the park and recreation field because the recreation leader must be able to understand the problems of the neighborhood and community and be able to communicate with the residents. Ethnic and racial balance in personnel greatly enhances the effectiveness of local park and recreation systems.

In a study conducted by the National Recreation and Park Association and the American Association for Health, Physical Education, Recreation, and Dance, 980 agencies throughout the United States were surveyed to determine the number of disadvantaged workers in local public park and recreation agencies. Twenty-one distinct job classifications were listed. The study revealed that disadvantaged workers held approximately 13 percent of the full-time jobs in parks and recreation and 25 percent of the part-time positions, most of which were seasonal jobs.

More than half of the disadvantaged workers employed in park and recreation agencies were in occupational categories of semi- or nonskilled personnel, such as facility supervisor, semiskilled park personnel, attendants and aides, and certain clerical positions. Of those occupying part-time and seasonal positions, the majority was in the category of attendants and aides. When the information from this study was compared to the information from a similar study done in 1967, the comparison showed a substantial employment increase in the categories of recreation program leaders, attendants and aides, activity specialists, facility supervisors, and park rangers.

In the same study it was found that a little more than 1 percent of park and recreation employees are disabled. Of these, about three out of ten are professionals, while the other seven out of ten are in nonprofessional jobs. The Americans with Disabilities Act has institutionalized a major change. Individuals can no longer be discriminated against for a position because of a disability. An applicant who is qualified, with or without reasonable accommodation, can perform the essential functions of the position. Reasonable accommodation may include, but is not limited to:

- Making existing facilities readily accessible to and usable by persons with disabilities.
- Restructuring the job, modifying work schedules, and reassigning the worker to a vacant position.
- Acquiring or modifying equipment or devices; adjusting or modifying examinations, training materials, or policies; and providing qualified readers or interpreters.

Salaries

Salaries relating to specific situations are supplied in the worker profiles found in Chapter 8; the information in this chapter will give you an idea of what salaries are possible. Salaries for full-time recreation positions range from approximately $12,000 to more than $70,000 per year. This is understandable because of the great variety of positions in this field. The salary scale for positions in municipal programs (the largest employment area in recreation) parallel rather closely the salaries for public school teachers in the same geographic area. This means that beginning salaries for employees with a bachelor's degree would range from $24,000 to $35,000 for twelve months. The same is true for jobs with youth agencies and hospitals.

Those employed by the federal government in recreation positions would receive salaries comparable to other federal employees of the same experience and rating. These are civil service jobs, and the salaries are determined by the civil service pay scale. Generally, federal employees in the field of recreation would receive between $18,000 and $40,000 per year. A few of the top positions would pay more. Recreation specialists employed in state government positions would also receive salaries comparable to their counterparts at the state level. Typically, state government employees receive $1,000 to $2,000 less per year than their federal government counterparts.

Faculty members in university recreation departments have salaries that cover the range of university faculty members in general. A typical salary for a young teacher with a master's degree and the rank of instructor would be $28,000 per year. A professor with a doctoral degree and the rank of associate professor would earn about $40,000. A professionally mature and expert faculty member holding a doctorate and the rank of full professor will earn $50,000 or more per year. Department heads of some of the better-recognized departments would receive several thousand per year more than this.

The highest paid people in the profession are the executives of large municipal programs. The one in charge of the program in a city of one million population, for example, would receive a salary of more than $55,000.

The summer salaries of student employees would be $5.35 to $10.00 per hour, and the same would be true for year-round part-time employees. However, summer positions that pay considerably better than this are available to better-prepared employees, such as schoolteachers.

Commercial recreation positions are the most difficult to interpret from the standpoint of salary expectations. These are like other private enterprise positions, meaning that the salary and the future success of the employee depend largely on the profit margin and the stability of the organization.

Looking for a Position

In the past, the public was accustomed to relying on volunteers for recreation leadership. Today, recreation professionals are valuable and deserve monetary rewards for their hard work. Recreation professionals are now being employed at all levels of government (see Appendix B). Federal and state government positions are not as numerous as jobs in local governments, but they have increased significantly in recent years. It appears that the number of federal and state positions will remain fairly stable in the near future. This is due to public pressure to limit the expansion of governmental services and to decrease the escalation of government spending.

Local government positions in city, county, and district recreation agencies constitute a major source of employment ranging all the way from direct leaders to departmental administrators. Increasingly, professionals are becoming employed by such commercial recreation enterprises as private golf courses, ski resorts, tennis clubs, theme parks, private camps, beach and boating resorts, sports clubs, health spas, as well as housing and condominium complexes. Other agencies that employ recreation leaders who possess specific qualifications are hospitals (therapeutic recreation), correctional institutions, the military, industrial/corporate organizations, and voluntary youth service agencies.

Federal Government Employment

In the past, most federal agencies have given primary attention to graduates whose educational emphasis was in the biological sciences; however, personnel with majors in recreation, social science, physical science, liberal arts, physical education, landscape architecture, and engineering also have been hired. The present philosophy of government administrators seems to favor personnel with dual talents who can effectively relate people to resource settings. They want professionals who are competent in working with all kinds of natural and man-made areas to make the best use of their aesthetic, functional, and economic potential. But more importantly, the professionals must always be aware that the areas are for people.

Because the awareness of the recreation profession is fairly recent, federal government positions are still based predominantly on natural resources. This is changing with military recreation and other services, and agencies employ many recreational professionals. One such agency is the National Park Service.

National Park Service

The National Park Service (NPS) administrates a system of national parks and similar reservations designated by statute, and national monuments and similar sites proclaimed by the president. It is an important federal employer. The agency has a permanent staff of more than seven thousand year-round employees who manage almost 459 national park areas throughout the nation. For those entering the NPS, employment opportunities are available in the following positions: park manager, park ranger, park guide and naturalist, historian, archaeologist, and designer, as well as many others. Long-time NPS employees hold most of the administrative positions. The park service hires numerous summer employees; a person contemplating a National Park Service career ought to have at least one summer of park service employment while pursuing his or her education.

The NPS selects its employees from the Civil Service Commission's list of candidates who have scored high on the Professional and Administrative Career Exam. Interested applicants may obtain a copy of the examination announcement covering the position in which they are interested at the local post office, at an office of the

Civil Service Commission, or by writing the NPS Headquarters, Department of the Interior, Washington, DC.

U.S. Forest Service

The U.S. Forest Service, a division of the Department of Agriculture, employs a large number of resource management personnel. A small proportion of these employees are involved primarily in the planning and management of outdoor recreation. Schools of forestry at several universities now offer specialization in outdoor recreation (see Appendix A), and graduates of these programs constitute the main source of recreation personnel hired by the U.S. Forest Service. With the national forests being used more and more for recreation, there will continue to be a steady increase in demand for competent forest recreation personnel. Like the NPS, the U.S. Forest Service selects its employees from candidates identified through the Civil Service Commission. Information about examination procedures may be obtained from the local post office, from any district or regional forest service office, or by writing directly to the U.S. Forest Service, Department of Agriculture, Washington, DC.

Additional Federal Government Opportunities

Other federal agencies that offer limited opportunities for employment in outdoor recreation are the U.S. Fish and Wildlife Service, the Bureau of Reclamation, the U.S. Army Corps of Engineers, the Bureau of Land Management, and the Tennessee Valley Authority. All of these are large resource management agencies whose areas receive extensive recreational use by the public. Therefore, recreation planning and management have become the responsibility of each of these agencies. For current federal position openings, visit www.usajob.opm.gov.

State Government Positions

A few decades ago the state park systems were meager in most states and received relatively few visitors: in 1960, state parks numbered 1,900, and received 100 million visitors; and in 1970, the number of parks had increased to 2,800, receiving 310 million visitors annually. But by the 2002, there were approximately 5,655 state parks with well over 758 million annual visits. This trend is indicative of demands being placed on state fish and wildlife divisions, natural resource management agencies, and other divisions of state governments involved in outdoor resource management.

In recent years, our better and more popular recreation areas have been strained to the limit, which threatens the sites. Federal and state legislators have recognized this and have taken rather bold measures to correct the situation through development of the areas and employment of more individuals better qualified in leadership.

Every state has a department that manages the state park system, and some of these departments also offer recreation consultation services. Additionally, every state has a wildlife management agency and departments or divisions that manage other state-owned natural resources. Further, every state has a tourism office as well as a designated person or office that coordinates the state's recreation functions with the NPS.

Some, but not all, of the personnel in these state departments and divisions are prepared professionally in recreation. Despite the fact that these jobs are not the exclusive domain of recreation professionals, there are several agencies in state governments that have significant responsibilities in recreation, providing some opportunities for employment of specialists in the field.

The positions are relatively few in each state, with the more populated states generally providing better employment opportunities. The state civil service office processes the applicants who fill most state positions of this kind. However, it is beneficial to also contact the particular department of government where you wish to be employed to be sure that your interests and qualifications are known. Applications and announcements are available at employment offices or by contacting your local state civil service office.

Local Government Opportunities

Local government recreation leaders can be divided into four general categories: administrators (executives), supervisors, center or special facility directors, and direct leaders. Principal employers are county, city, and township parks and recreation divisions. Each division has its own hiring process and organizational structure.

Most local governmental agencies establish county parks and recreation divisions to manage the county parks. Their focus is on the site and simply maintaining any recreational activity available at that site, for example, offering canoe rentals or monitoring fishing piers. Employees are usually hired through the County Human Resources Department.

City agencies actively implement and manage both aspects of parks and recreation. Living in a city with an established division offers residents opportunities to use groomed city or specialty parks, enroll in enrichment and educational recreational programs, and participate in city activity and sports leagues. Employment availability is based on the established type of city government. A mayor-council government appoints a parks and recreation director, who hires his or her staff. The department's employment is based on the mayoral election every four years. If a new council and a new mayor are elected, they have the right to appoint a new director, who, in turn, may hire new staff members. If the city is run by a city manager-council, the council employs the manager, the manager hires the director, and the director determines the staff. If the manager changes, the parks and recreation director and staff remain the same, and employment is based on merit.

Township parks and recreation divisions are often determined based on size and the needs of the community. Communities that function under a township government tend to be larger in population and do not fall within a city's geographical boundaries. Needs arise because unlike those who live within the city limits, the residents of townships are not offered the benefits of unconditional use of city parks and recreation. So, public land under the jurisdiction of the township may be developed into small or neighborhood parks; and the township parks and recreation department takes the responsibility to maintain, develop, and acquire the land for leisure pursuits, playground equipment, or township activities. Recreation may include resident enrichment programs, special populations programming, and special events within the community. Employment is determined much like city government. The director and staff may be appointed or hired.

A Word of Caution

Even though the future of the recreation and park profession appears generally aggressive and optimistic, it is important to understand that this field does not present a plethora of employment opportunities. Like any profession, there are gains and losses. For example, after 9/11, airlines reported cutbacks and layoffs, and hurricanes affected East Coast and Florida tourism. The profession will undoubtedly experience consistent growth and improved status, but the growth and improvement will not be as dramatic as some have predicted.

During the past decade, the market for college trained recreation and park personnel has expanded at a steady and healthy rate, and there is no reason to expect that this trend will change. In view of the recent past, the following points are important:

1. Those who want to make a career of this field need to prepare themselves expertly so they can compete in the job market.
2. The leaders of the profession need to strive for more effective development and enforcement of standards and procedures that will enhance the employment of those who have prepared themselves well for leadership positions.

8

Profiles of Professionals

Leisure is intrinsically bound up in the quality of life. Its distribution, among the population and over lifetimes, and the uses to which it is put are indicative of the well-being of a society. Yet, the growth of available leisure time in this country has been less widely noted than a corresponding growth in the output of goods and services, perhaps because of its elusive quality.
— J. D. Hodgson, former Secretary of Labor

THE FOLLOWING ARE descriptions of typical situations in which individuals have been successful in leisure occupations. These success stories purposely cover a broad range of jobs and exemplify various avenues by which people become employed in recreation-related positions. There are many other examples that could be cited, but these give a fairly broad spectrum of the leadership opportunities in this field.

Public Service

William Freeman is assistant director of a state parks department in a western state that administers approximately seventy-six state park and recreation areas. He is a state civil service employee with more than sixteen years of tenure with the state parks department and has been assistant director for about ten years. Mr. Freeman holds a bachelor's degree in recreation and park planning and a master's degree in public administration. Before his employment by the state, he had several years of experience as an employee of a ski resort during the winter months.

Paul Pearson is the director of recreation for a community of approximately twenty-seven thousand residents. During the summer, the municipal program is expanded to include a large variety of activities with an emphasis on youth; therefore, numerous part-time employees are hired. During the school year, the program is reduced to a more minimal level with a small staff. Mr. Pearson has the same fringe benefits as other city employees. Prior to his present position, he was a physical education teacher and athletic coach in the public schools. Mr. Pearson holds a bachelor's degree in physical education and a master's degree in recreation administration. It was after obtaining the master's degree that he moved from education into recreation administration.

George Adamson is a superintendent of recreation and parks for a city in the Midwest of approximately a half million people. He has had a variety of experience in the profession. He was a schoolteacher for two years then took a job in the recreation field, earning a master's degree while continuing full-time employment. In his present position, he administers a program that employs a full-time year-round staff of 150 workers. He enjoys the desirable fringe benefits of administrative employees. Mr. Adamson has had a very significant influence on the development of his community and is well-known and respected in the city. In addition, he is well-known in the profession and has had significant influence on its development at both the regional and national levels.

Myron Hogan is the grounds supervisor of a large city park in a populous area. Mr. Hogan holds an associate degree in horticulture from a community college, and prior to obtaining his present position, he worked with the city parks department as a park maintenance man. It was during this time that he went to college part-time and earned the associate degree.

Susan Jolley is an aquatic specialist who works in a municipal swim program. She graduated with an associate degree in recreation from a nearby junior college. Because of her long-time interest and participation in aquatic activities, including competitive swimming, she is qualified as a swimming instructor and as a supervisor of aquatics. As a full-time employee, she has the same fringe benefits as other city employees.

Laurie Archuleta Jerge received her master's degree in human performance and sport from New Mexico Highlands University and her bachelor's degree in leisure administration. After graduating, Laurie became the program director for the Roswell Family YMCA. She is currently the recreation program analyst for the city of Roswell and is a certified leisure professional. She is better known as the "Voice of Roswell Recreation," as she educates and informs the public on the benefits of recreation. In her position she analyzes and assists in the development and the promotion of community recreation activities for Roswell. Laurie hosts a television program entitled *Leisure Living* that is produced by N.M.M.I. Television Productions. She regularly provides information and public service announcements to the *Roswell Daily Record* and is scheduled frequently on four local radio stations, where she promotes the parks and recreation movement in the Roswell community. Laurie is heard daily on local radio with the "Roswell Recreation Report." She believes that the media's support has allowed her to bring to the forefront the importance of the role of leisure education, and she is extremely grateful to them for the opportunity. She assists with special events and is responsible for the evaluation of programs and services. Laurie has been known to say that "To change someone's life for the better, to me, is the ultimate reward; the purpose behind the determination."

Evan Stephenson is a director of a college student union on the campus of a state university with a student body of about ninety-five hundred. Management of the student union includes food services, a student union activities program, and student body officer leadership. Mr. Stephenson earned a bachelor's degree in sociology and, after three years of employment as a social worker, went back to college and earned a master's degree in recreation administration. Following two years of experience as a teacher on the recreational faculty at a junior college, he accepted his present position, where he has the potential of a good future or the possibility of moving into a higher-level management position at the university. His fringe benefits are the same as those that other university employees receive.

Margaret Murphy is an associate professor in the Department of Recreation and Park Administration at a university in the Midwest. Prior to becoming a university professor, Ms. Murphy had three years of experience on the staff of a youth service agency, was on the staff of a community center, and was a supervisor in a municipal recreation program. During her undergraduate college years, she worked summers at a youth camp and in a municipal recreation program. Professor Murphy has completed her doctorate degree.

She keeps well informed on facts and concepts relating to her profession. To enhance her professional preparation and overall contributions, she has remained active in professional organizations and community affairs.

Lyon Allredge, assistant superintendent of schools in an Arizona community of approximately 210,000 residents, has the specific responsibility of administering the community school program. This program is based on the concept of making thorough community use of school facilities. Much of the use is in the form of recreational activities during out-of-school hours. Mr. Allredge obtained a bachelor's degree in education and taught in the public schools for three years before returning to the university, where he earned a master's degree in community school administration. His future appears bright because his position is stable, his future salary will be in accordance with the local school district pay scale, and the fringe benefits and working conditions are desirable. In the future, he may find an opportunity to move to a similar position in a larger organization, or he might someday become a school principal or the superintendent of schools in his present community.

Ilene Parker is a civilian recreation employee at a naval base on the West Coast. Having served as a recreation employee with the armed forces for eleven years, she has been on the staff at three different military stations, two in the United States and one in Europe. She has desirable fringe benefits and a bright future with the federal service. Prior to entering civil service employment, Ms. Parker worked in a municipal recreation program: first as an activities specialist, then as a recreation center director, and later as supervisor of a geographic region within the municipal program.

Robert Saffrine is stationed at Teton National Park in Jackson, Wyoming, as a park planner employed with the National Park Service. His bachelor's degree was in landscape architecture and horticulture, and he has been employed by the park service with a civil service rating of GS-8. He enjoys all the fringe benefits associated with civil service employment in addition to the benefit of low-rent federal housing. Being a dedicated outdoorsman and an advocate of preservation and conservative use of natural resources for the enjoyment of people, Mr. Saffrine is pleased with his contribution to society and finds his work very satisfying. At a relatively young age, he is well established with the federal service and plans to continue as a national park employee.

Trina Peligreno is a therapeutic recreation specialist in a veterans hospital on the eastern seaboard. Ms. Peligreno earned a bachelor's degree from a state college in New York with a major in prephysical therapy. Rather than going into physical therapy, she decided to earn a master's degree in therapeutic recreation. Extending her master's degree education over a two-year period, she was able to work part-time as a therapeutic recreation assistant in a children's hospital. Upon completion of the degree, she was employed full-time for two years at the children's hospital as a recreation therapist before joining the staff at the veterans hospital. Ms. Peligreno thoroughly enjoys working with hospital patients, and she feels she serves an excellent purpose in adding interest to their lives and helping with their rehabilitation.

Private Sector

Sema Nicholic currently is employed as the tennis professional (head instructor) at a private tennis club in Florida. He came to the United States in 1968 from Yugoslavia to attend college on a tennis scholarship. He spent four years as a successful member of the tennis team while improving his skills in the English language and earning a bachelor's degree in a noncertification physical education program. Upon graduation he accepted a job as an assistant tennis professional at a private club in Georgia. After two years of experience and proving himself as an excellent instructor and a good organizer, he accepted the head professional position at the club in Florida, which included a substantial increase in salary. It seems likely that Nicholic will continue along this line of employment and, by doing so, will accomplish two important purposes: he will earn a very good living in a leisure occupation, and he will contribute much to the enjoyment and enrichment of those he teaches.

Mike Ranier is the golf professional at a medium-sized golf club in northern California. After spending a lot of time during his teenage years learning the game and developing a high level of skill, Ranier gained entrance onto a university golf team. There he perfected his game and learned much about instructional techniques. He earned a bachelor's degree, majoring in business management, with the idea that he would pursue golf instruction and golf course management as his profession. He supplements his salary with additional funds as a consultant and by playing in local tournaments.

John Martin is the director of a private swim club located in Philadelphia. Having been an outstanding competitive swimmer, his reputation and demonstrated competency attract a sufficient clientele within the membership of the club to sustain the program at a high level. In addition to earning a bachelor's degree with a major in physical education, he has had extensive experience in swimming competition and in teaching and training younger competitors. After graduating from college, Mr. Martin worked for two years as an assistant in a privately owned commercial swim school, after which he had two years' experience as a college-swim coach.

The future looks promising for him with respect to both earnings and professional status.

Dennis Marshall is supervisor of a recreation program sponsored by the employee association of a large industrial plant in Nashville, Tennessee. The association owns various facilities, which include a family-youth camp forty miles away and a park located near the industrial complex. The site encompassess a clubhouse, swimming facilities, athletic fields, and picnic areas. In addition to the activities sponsored at these two privately owned facilities, the program includes participation in such instructional and competitive activities as bowling and skating. Mr. Marshall became familiar with this position through his involvement as an industrial employee while working his way through college. Being a recreation major, he showed strong interest in recreation leadership at the plant. Upon graduation from college, he was able to work part-time in the plant while working as an assistant in the recreation program. After two years of this arrangement, he became director of the industrial recreation program. Even though he is an employee of the association and not the industrial company, arrangements have been made for him to receive all of the fringe benefits available to the industrial employees. Even though Mr. Marshall's present job does not offer great opportunity for advancement, it is a substantial position that offers a good future. Further, it is providing good preparation for moving to more lucrative employment of the same kind with another organization.

George Eubank is an aggressive and ambitious young man who taught on a university faculty for two years following graduation from a master's degree program. After deciding not to make a career of teaching, he entered the commercial recreation field as a limited partner and assistant manager of Outdoor Recreation Unlimited

(ORU), a regional hunting and fishing organization. ORU conducts hunting and fishing excursions, provides guide services, and sells memberships to people who want to hunt and fish on private lands where the organization has leased hunting and fishing rights. As in other private enterprises, Mr. Eubank will rise or fall with the success of the organization. Therefore, he must help the organization produce a profit on a regular basis, while at the same time building its assets, so it will become a more substantial enterprise. His job is primarily planning and promotional in nature.

Paul Allen is presently a district representative for a sports and recreation equipment and supply company. He graduated from college with undergraduate training in the areas of recreation and sociology. After working three years in a municipal recreation program, he returned to college and earned a master's degree in park and recreation administration. He then joined the state extension service at a land-grant university in the capacity of recreation and park specialist. After serving in this position for four years, he accepted his present position, which he finds exciting and challenging, and he believes it offers a very promising financial future.

Jan Eliason is an employee of a recreation travel agency that promotes and schedules various kinds of excursions, including river float-trips, scenic bus tours, charter air flights to vacation and resort areas, and the scheduling of hunting and fishing excursions in cooperation with outfitting and guide personnel. After completing high school, Ms. Eliason attended college for two and a half years, where she concentrated on secretarial training and office management. Following this, she was employed as a secretary for two years before becoming a full-time homemaker. She decided to re-enter full-time employment and did so by seeking out her present position. She is well prepared for her job because she has the necessary secretarial and management skills combined with an outgoing and enthusiastic personality. She has the ability to meet the public well and to interest them in the programs she represents. Additionally, Ms. Eliason has had a variety of travel experiences and is perceptive of the vacation and recreation travel interests of people.

See Appendix C for a list of various organizations that employ recreation professionals.

9

ORGANIZATIONS BENEFICIAL TO THE PROFESSION

He who knows all of the answers, ends up solving all of the problems by himself.

—Brett Vess

EXPERIENCE IS A key component to getting a position in the leisure field. Membership and participation in professional and service organizations related to the field is a proven method for obtaining experience. Involvement also provides opportunities to tap a vast circuit of knowledge and wisdom from those who have gone or go through similar situations.

There are many professional organizations associated with recreation and parks at the state, regional, and national levels. Every state has a state association for health, physical education, and recreation, as well as a recreation and park association or society. There are also district and national organizations that correspond to these. Further, there are state, district, and national organizations that relate only to specific areas of recreation and parks, such as camping, skiing, and boating. In this section, it is feasible to discuss briefly only a few of the more prominent national organizations. See Appendix D for a list of professional organizations.

The American Alliance for Health, Physical Education, Recreation, and Dance

The American Alliance for Health, Physical Education, Recreation, and Dance (AAHPERD) is a voluntary education organization made up of six national associations and six district associations with fifty-four state and territorial affiliates. The membership, which exceeds twenty-six thousand, is composed of health and physical educators, coaches and athletic directors, and personnel in safety, recreation and leisure services, and dance. The organization was founded in 1885 by a group of forty-nine people, mostly educators and physicians interested in promoting physical training. Today the membership network reaches into more than sixteen thousand school districts, two thousand colleges and universities, and ten thousand community recreation units.

These national associations belong to the alliance:

• **American Association for Leisure and Recreation (AALR).** Promotes school, community, and national programs of leisure services and recreation education.

• **American Association for Health Education (AAHE).** Works for continuing, comprehensive programs of health education. Position papers are developed on such health topics as certification, drug education, and sex education.

• **National Association for Girls and Women in Sport (NAGWS).** Serves those involved in teaching, coaching, officiating, athletic administration, athletic training, club sports, and intra-murals at the elementary, secondary, and college levels.

• **National Association for Sport and Physical Education (NASPE).** Provides leadership opportunities in physical education and sports development, competition, consultation, publications, conferences, research, and a public information program.

• **National Dance Association (NDA).** Promotes the development of sound policies for dance in education through conferences, convention programs, special projects, publications, and cooperation with other dance and art groups.

• **American Association for Active Lifestyles and Fitness (AAALF).** Serves professionals facilitating programs of physical activity and fitness, and the instructors who train them. AAALF acts as an advocate for underrepresented populations and interests.

AAHPERD holds a national convention each year. In addition, each of the six districts holds a district convention annually, and the fifty-four state and territorial affiliates also conduct annual conventions. The alliance and its affiliates sponsor a large number of workshops, conferences, and clinics each year. All of these are pointed toward professional development of the members or the solution of particular issues pertaining to the profession. AAHPERD also conducts a job placement service.

The alliance produces five regular publications: *Update*; *Strategies*; *American Journal of Health Educators*; *Journal of Physical Education, Recreation, and Dance*; and the *Research Quarterly for Exercise and Sport*. Also, more than a dozen newsletters are prepared and distributed to provide information in specific areas of the associations. The alliance publishes fifty to sixty books and films each year, the titles of which are available in AAHPERD's publications catalog. The home office of the alliance is located at

1900 Association Drive, Reston, Virginia 20191-1598. The website is www.aahperd.org.

American Camping Association

The American Camping Association (ACA) was established in 1910 to further the welfare of children and adults of America through camping and to extend the recreational and educational benefits of out-of-doors living. The association serves as the voice of more than sixty-six hundred members throughout the nation, and it is the organization that stimulates high professional standards among camp leaders and camping agencies. It sponsors national conferences for the purpose of improving camp leadership and camp programs.

ACA publishes *Camping Magazine* bimonthly and publishes and distributes several books and pamphlets on camping and related activities. It is financed through membership dues. The home office address is 5000 State Road, 67 North, Martinsville, Indiana 46151-7902. The website is www.acacamps.org.

Canadian Association for Health, Physical Education, Recreation, and Dance

The Canadian Association for Health, Physical Education, Recreation, and Dance (CAHPERD) is the Canadian counterpart for AAHPERD. CAHPERD is a national nonprofit voluntary organization that, since its inception in 1933, has been concerned and engaged in providing and extending the benefits of physical activity to the citizens of Canada. Its particular objectives are:

1. To acquire and disseminate knowledge pertaining to physical activity of human beings

2. To stimulate interest and participation in physical activity by all Canadians
3. To promote the establishment of acceptable programs of physical activity under the direction of qualified leaders
4. To participate actively in the establishment and the improvement of standards of practice of all who are entrusted with the responsibility of leadership in the fields of physical activity
5. To encourage relationships among professional groups concerned with human physical activity
6. To cooperate with any and all local, provincial, national, and international organizations committed to the improvement of the well-being of people

CAHPERD issues a monthly periodical and a quarterly research bulletin, and it publishes numerous pamphlets and booklets on various topics of the profession. The national office is at 2197 Riverside Drive, Suite 403, Ottawa, Ontario, Canada K1H 7X3. The website is www.cahperd.ca.

Employee Services Management Association

The Employee Services Management Association (ESM) was formerly known as the National Industrial Recreation Association (NIRA). ESM is a nonprofit organization dedicated to the principle that employee recreation, fitness, and other service programs are essential to effective personnel management. The members of the association are the suppliers and directors of such programs in business, industry, and the government. ESM originated in 1941 and today serves more than two thousand member companies in the United States and Canada. Its official publication is *Employee*

Services Management Magazine, which reaches five thousand industries six times a year. Further, the association holds annual conferences at the national and regional levels for the purpose of disseminating useful information and updating its members on current trends and new program ideas.

ESM promotes employee programs as a means of improving productivity and fostering good relations among the employees and between employees and management. It assists member organizations in developing, promoting, and improving recreation and other non-negotiated employee benefits.

In addition to its bimonthly magazine and annual conferences, it distributes newsletters, provides product and service discounts for employee groups, disseminates program ideas, and provides consultation. It facilitates three national award programs each year. For more information, contact ESM Association, 2211 York Road, Suite 207, Oak Brook, Illinois 60523-2371. Or visit its website at www.esmassn.org.

National Recreation and Park Association

The National Recreation and Park Association (NRPA) is an independent, nonprofit service organization dedicated to the conservation of natural resources; the beautification of the environment; and the development, expansion, and improvement of park and recreation leadership, programs, facilities, and services for human growth and community betterment. NRPA is the only independent national organization servicing all aspects of the nation's park and recreation movement. Much of its income is raised through membership dues.

NRPA was formed in 1966 by the merger of five pioneer organizations in the park and recreation field: the American Association of Zoological Parks and Aquariums, the American Institute of Park Executives, the American Recreation Society, the National Conference on State Parks, and the National Recreation Association. It has a professional staff located at the headquarters office in Virginia. Additional professionals associated with the organization are found through fifty-seven national and state affiliates.

To serve each member's special interests, NRPA has eight branches: the Armed Forces Recreation Society, the American Park and Recreation Society, the Citizen-Board Member Branch, the National Society for Park Resources, the Student Branch, the National Therapeutic Recreation Society, the National Aquatic Branch, and the Society of Park and Recreation Educators.

NRPA services are generally classified into five primary categories, although some overlap the others: (1) public affairs, (2) research, (3) professional services, (4) membership, and (5) executive. It also provides a webpage with career openings.

The association sponsors numerous annual educational and planning conferences and workshops on national and regional levels. It prepares and distributes books and pamphlets on park and recreation topics. It also produces the following publications:

1. *Parks and Recreation* (monthly). A magazine designed to acquaint the general public with various park and recreation problems, trends, ideas, and policies.
2. *Journal of Park and Recreation Administration* (quarterly). Provides analysis of management and theoretical practices and research.

3. A series of "how-to" manuals dealing with specific policy and management functions.
4. *Schole.* The annual publication of the Society of Park and Recreation Educators. It offers information related to courses, curricula, and teaching.
5. A publications and resources catalog that provides an annotated list of recreation books available for purchase through NRPA's book center.
6. A regular series of monthly, bimonthly, and quarterly newsletters on topics of specific interest to professionals and lay board members in the park and recreation field.
7. *Journal of Leisure Research* (quarterly). Highlights the most recent and pertinent research efforts in parks and recreation.
8. *Therapeutic Recreation Journal* (quarterly). Contains articles of interest to members of the National Therapeutic Recreation Society.
9. *Dateline.* A monthly newsletter for all members.

The home office of NRPA is located at 22377 Belmont Ridge Road, Ashburn, Virginia 20148. The website is www.nrpa.org.

10

IMPRINTS OF
A CHANGING SOCIETY

You may be on the right track, but you'll still get ran over if you just sit there.

—Roy Rogers

AMERICANS SPEND ABOUT a third of their income on leisure pursuits. In the 1990s, consumers spent approximately $280 billion on recreational goods and services, constituting about 7 percent of all consumer spending. This figure is expected to continue to rise. Leisure and related agencies have become the number-one industry in the United States.

In light of the fact that recreation and leisure job opportunities are prominent, it is especially important that prospective members of the occupational field be well informed about recent changes and present trends, including both the positive and negative aspects.

Following are explanations of some of the more important changes and trends.

Government Restraints

Local government recreation and park agencies have constituted the mainstream of employment in the area of recreation and park management. Further, the number of such agencies and their ability to employ recreation leaders has increased tremendously since World War II, with the fastest rate of increase occurring during the 1960s and early 1970s. This increase has been the main contributing factor to the tremendous expansion of recreation and park major programs in colleges and universities. It is a fact, however, that during the 1980s, municipal recreation and park programs remained at a fairly constant level, meaning there was very little increase in job opportunities in these programs during that decade.

Also, leisure employment in federal and state agencies remained at near the same level during the decade of the 1980s. This is because of public pressure for reduced government spending and nonexpansion of government services. Not much has changed since then. With a $413 billion federal deficit reported in September 2004, layoffs and hiring freezes for many programs have occurred. Recently, agencies that depend on the government for financing operations and personnel are looking to more creative means to maintain their current staffing and budget. Partnerships, sponsorships, donations, and mergers help reduce financial strain.

Travel

It appears that the increased cost of travel is here to stay, and this is having a curtailing effect on the amount of travel that people do for all purposes. Consequently, jobs that relate to the tourist industry have increased at a slower rate than earlier predictions. The rate of gradual increase will likely continue during the foreseeable future, and this will have a particular effect on resort areas and recreation places far away from the population.

Four-Day Workweek

There has been a considerable amount of experimentation in American industry with the four-day workweek. In most cases, the four-day workweek consists of ten-hour days, so that the total for the week is still forty hours. But some companies have gone to a thirty-six-hour week made up of four nine-hour days. The American Management Association reported that of the companies it surveyed, 6 percent were involved with the four-day workweek either for all or part of their employees. Another 18 percent were studying the four-day workweek but had not yet decided to implement it. One percent had experimented with it and then discarded the idea. This means that approximately 25 percent of the companies surveyed by the AMA were either involved with a four-day workweek or were considering adopting it.

Population Shifts

Currently slightly more than three-fourths of the people in America live in urban and suburban areas. In the year 2000, 79 percent of the 281 million people lived in these areas. Parts of the East Coast, Great Lakes, the West Coast, and the southern Gulf Coast region each represent a sprawling metropolis. Also, the Rocky Mountains region and the Sunbelt area of the Southwest are much more populated than they have been.

Recently, there has been an indication of a shift from suburbs to cities in the middle-class and upper-class residential areas. Undoubtedly this has been encouraged by traffic congestion and the increased costs of commuting, and the trend is having a stimulating effect on the rehabilitation of urban areas.

Another noticeable shift of population is from the industrial areas of the East and Midwest to the Sunbelt regions of the South and Southwest. This is partly influenced by employment opportunities and partly by the migration of retirees, which, in turn, helps to stimulate employment opportunities in the Sunbelt region.

Technological Advances

During recent decades we have had great advances in technology, and these advances have influenced practically every aspect of our lives, including what we do for recreation, where we do it, and how much time we spend doing it. In the future, technology will have even greater effects on recreation patterns. New devices used for participation will continue to develop, and the further advancement of technology will open new worlds of leisure time activities. Technology will be both a friend and an enemy to recreation because, while it will enhance recreation participation, it also will be destructive to certain portions of the recreation environment. Air pollution, water pollution, land pollution, and acid rain result partly from the industrialized aspect of modern technology.

Resource Supply

The supply of basic resources (namely land and water) for recreation will not increase. Certain modifications and improvements can enhance the usefulness of some of the resources, but such revisions have limited potential. On the other hand, there seems to be no limit to the potential increase in demands on the resources, and it is well established that the demands will escalate at an ever-increasing rate. This simple relationship between supply and demand means that in the future we will need to: (1) more thoroughly identify the areas of high recreation potential and prevent the needed resources from being committed on a permanent basis to less essential uses; (2) continue at an increased rate to alter and improve certain resources so that they will better serve the increased demands; and (3) modify our participation in recreation activities to a level that can be accommodated by the available resources.

Future Participation Trends

During recent years the overall participation in recreation activities has increased about 50 percent faster than the population. This has been due to several influencing factors that have already been discussed, primarily increased leisure time, increased means, and a more favorable philosophy toward participation in recreational activities.

Naturally, there will be changes in the popularity of different recreation activities and some new forms of participation will become possible due to technology. For the most part, the changes will be moderate and the emphasis will continue to be on the simple and traditional forms of recreation such as hiking, cycling, camping, swimming, cultural events, and athletic participation. However, there will be a continued increase in high-risk activities (river running, skydiving, hang gliding, rock climbing); winter sports, especially snowboarding and snowmobiling; water sports, particularly wind surfing, waterskiing, and underwater exploration;

health-related activities with emphasis upon physical fitness; and wilderness experiences.

Beaches and waterways are particularly attractive for recreation, and the population tends to cluster along these areas for reasons of both commerce and recreation. Because of this, proper use and management of beaches and water corridors will be of crucial importance in the future. It is also true that areas of great beauty and unique natural features will continue to grow in popularity at a disproportionate rate. Unfortunately, many of these have fragile features that must be protected from abuse and overuse.

With people's increased awareness about the need to maintain an acceptable level of physical fitness and health, leisure time will become increasingly occupied by activities that promote fitness. There will be more runners, more cyclists, more golfers, and more participants in virtually every popular form of fitness activity. One hopes there will also be more emphasis on other aspects of the healthy life such as weight control and discretion in the use of tobacco, alcohol, drugs, and other harmful substances.

There is recognition of the need to broaden the recreation program content in the area of the cultural arts and to utilize more fully the personnel in organizations within the community to expand and improve cultural arts opportunities. The emphasis on creativity as a desirable use of leisure time will have an increasing positive effect resulting in more extensive participation in and a greater number of cultural activities.

Recently, there has been an upsurge in private campgrounds, luxury marinas, tennis complexes, resort villages, hunting and fishing preserves, and amusement complexes such as Disneyworld and Marineland. Future technology will contribute to continued change with the prospects of plastic snow and ice for skiing and skating, double- and triple-deck golf driving ranges, artificial surfs for swimming and surfing, artificial white-water courses, programmed travel packages, underwater exploration vehicles, and a multitude of other leisure time innovations.

All told, the most useful and most used recreation areas and facilities will be those close to the population; places that can be reached conveniently on a daily and weekend basis without excessive travel and expense. The majority of the population will concentrate on recreational opportunities that are convenient and close at hand.

Successful Leadership

It is generally agreed that there is no substitute for strong, innovative leadership. Regardless of what else is done by way of support, the results of an organization or a program will not exceed the level of its leadership.

Leadership preparation in the leisure sciences must enable individuals to deal successfully with rapidly changing leisure options. Within one future life span, recreation seems destined to be more varied and dynamic than at any equal time in the past. Young professionals who are now entering the field will likely be engaged beyond the year 2034. It is obviously important to develop young leaders who are versatile and who will furnish adequate leadership over a long period under rapidly changing circumstances. It seems certain that our world thirty years in the future will be even more unlike the world of today than today is different from the world of thirty years ago.

On the surface it appears that professional leadership preparation is the responsibility of colleges and universities, but this is only partially true because the growth and development of profession-als must be continuous. This comes about with valuable on-the-job experience, some of which must be in the form of in-service train-ing such as conferences, institutes, and clinics; regular reading of professional literature; volunteering; and tutoring from those who are professionally more mature and better informed.

The leadership in recreation will need to come from a combi-nation of well-prepared resource management specialists (to plan and manage parks and natural resources), recreation programming specialists, and a multitude of others who are specialized in such areas as landscape architecture, horticulture, wildlife, cultural arts, sports education, travel, and numerous other interests that con-tribute to the recreational fulfillment of the population.

Some of the most important leaders in the future will be con-noisseurs who have broad perspectives and keen insights into cul-tural change and individual tastes and preferences. Such leaders will have to demonstrate an accurate feel for the interests of people and for the wise use of resources for both the immediate and long-term future.

Other Trends and Changes

Education for the worthy use of leisure will become an even more important responsibility of schools and other educational agencies. Creative and ingenious leadership will be required in connection with program and class content.

There will be a strong trend toward increased use of schools and other public facilities for recreational activities when the facilities are not in use for their primary purposes.

We will see significant increases in employment for recreation specialists in corrective institutions; private club employees such as golf, tennis, and swimming instructors; managers and programmers at resorts; recreation directors for large condominium complexes and retirement villages; leaders of industrial recreation programs; and program leaders for special populations (senior citizens, single adult, handicapped).

The market for services, supplies, and equipment used in leisure activities will boom, and this will result in considerable expansion of job opportunities in leisure-related manufacturing and business.

Jobs with such voluntary youth agencies as the YMCA and YWCA and boys and girls clubs will continue to increase as in the recent past.

There will be an accelerated trend toward creativity in the design of playgrounds, play equipment, and recreational centers. Standard equipment and facility designs that have been with us for a long time will become obsolete.

The professional qualifications of job candidates will increase as fast as the supply of qualified personnel will permit. Thus there will be a steady trend for job applicants to have better credentials. In response to this, professional preparation programs will become more stringent. This, in turn, will cause college major programs to become more standardized, and they will be subjected to accreditation by regional and national accrediting agencies.

One of the adjustments that is taking place and will continue in the future is a more even spread of facility use during the week as compared to weekends. This is due to a combination of factors including: (1) the increased percentage of the population that is retired or partially retired and whose time availability is the same on Tuesday as on Saturday; (2) later entry by youth into the job market and more availability of discretionary time by youth; (3) the trend toward more involvement with the four-day workweek; and (4) the continued reduction in the average workweek (it is now about thirty-six hours for the majority of the nation's full-time employees).

With the attitude toward more stringent controls on government spending, and with projected continued financial affluence, there will be a marked increase in commercialized recreation. Those with good business minds will find many opportunities to capitalize on people's leisure time interests in terms of financial profit. One hopes they will demonstrate sound judgment about what is good for society and keep exploitation of people, the environment, and resources to a minimum. The recreation professionals will have to guard against such imbalances along the way. This can be done by bringing community pressure against undesirable commercialism and by sponsoring appealing programs through community agencies that will combat the popularizing of undesirable commercial activities.

Leisure Counseling

It appears that sometime in the foreseeable future, leisure counseling will become a branch of the profession. The counseling will be primarily in the form of helping people review the leisure time segment of their lives and which alternatives are open to them in view of their particular skills, interests, and financial status. The counselor will help people crystallize their thinking about what they would like to do, what they want to become in terms of leisure time participants, and how they can go about achieving their objectives. Another aspect will be the counseling of people who have particular physical, social, and psychological problems of a kind that leisure time activities can help solve.

An accelerated research effort will be needed to accumulate the information that will be necessary to give appropriate direction to the various facets of the leisure time movement. Much of the research will take place on college and university campuses. But some of it will be conducted through nonschool agencies.

Stretching the Mind

In two or three decades from now, another author will be able to write about changes that are equally as dramatic as the changes currently experienced. He or she may talk about sightseeing tours in outer space or excursions deep under the sea in capsules or glass submarines. That author may lament the plight of the wilderness hiker before the development of individualized flying devices that silently carry recreation participants to mountaintops and once remote fishing, hunting, and scenic areas. That writer may refer to new forms of computerized golf and baseball designed especially for less space. He or she will probably speak of the more affluent individuals who have personal counselors to help select and arrange leisure time pursuits and may even mention reservations made for those persons on Moon Flight 732.

These ideas may seem far-fetched, but not many years ago it would have been just as far-fetched to talk seriously about making twenty-five ski runs from the top of Beaver Mountain in one day, or taking a weekend hunting trip to Alaska, or waterskiing behind a powerboat traveling at thirty miles per hour.

It is possible that these futuristic projections are not really that far-fetched or, in fact, even that far away. Creativity, involvement, and knowledge by recreation professionals offer the only kind of limitations to the field. The prosperity of the occupation remains in the hands of people passionate about the wellness of society, the commodity of time, and the activities and opportunities available for people to grow. Where does your passion lie?

11

RECREATION CAREERS IN CANADA

This trip gave me a glimpse of Canada, an impression of its immensity and diversity . . . I left Canada thrilled with what I had seen, eager to return and to be somehow, at some time and in some place, a participant in the adventure of developing this land with its vast possibilities, so many of them still dormant, still undreamed—the romance of Canada.

— Tyrone Guthrie

CANADA HAS A great variety of settings for recreation and leisure pursuits, from national and state parks to recreation agencies and organizations. These opportunities are offered by municipal, provincial, or federal governments; by nonprofit organizations; or by commercial, corporate, outdoor, and open-space recreation agencies. Hospitals, senior citizens homes, and specialized agencies offer recreational programs for people with special needs.

A Changing Perspective

The overall trend shows that recreation spending is on the rise in Canada for all families with children, regardless of their level of income. More and more Canadian families want to ensure that they and their children have access to recreation services and opportunities. This aspect gives a new perspective not only about the need for recreational activities in Canada but also of the future employment opportunities in this field.

Leisure is a growing industry in Canada, and professionals are needed to provide quality recreation services to customers. Recreational professionals can to pursue careers in different agencies, and their jobs require different levels of knowledge, skills, and attitudes. Degree programs for studying recreation and leisure, and related areas, are available in thirty-four universities in Canada. They provide knowledge on the subject studied and practical experience in the field. Professionals with a degree in recreation and leisure studies can find a job easily in the field after graduation due to the broad variety of recreational and leisure settings. These settings include sport and active-living organizations, government agencies, nonprofit organizations, therapeutic and inclusive community recreation organizations, outdoors recreation organizations, travel and tourism organizations, and arts, culture, and heritage agencies.

In Canada, the level of training and specialization is going to be an important aspect in employment; more and more jobs will require a higher level of education and training, with a higher level of specialization. Many universities across Canada prepare their students for jobs in tourism, parks, outdoor recreation, entertainment, therapeutic recreation, and municipal and cultural recreation.

The average hourly wage for people employed in recreation and sport in Canada is somewhere around seventeen dollars. This is a wage that is similar to, and in some cases higher than, that made by people employed in sales and service, business, finance and administration, the trades, transport and equipment operations, primary industry and processing, and manufacturing and utilities.

Jobs in recreation and leisure services in Canada involve duties related to administration, programming, research, planning, and parks and facility management. Administration positions include recreation managers, directors, assistant directors, and municipal recreation and parks superintendents.

Aspects of the Profession

People employed in the occupations from this category have to plan, organize, control, and evaluate the operations of recreation programs and services. They are responsible for employee training, and they have to provide technical and professional advice on recreational and sports matters. They often have duties in directing fund-raising campaigns and public relations activities and organizing major events. For a position in a recreation and sports program, candidates must have a university degree in recreation management or a related field, several years of experience in an occupation related to recreation and sports administration, and consulting or programming skills. Some directors of recreation may be required to have a Municipal Recreation Director's Certificate.

Executive directors of sports governing agencies may be required to have coaching certification in a particular sport. The salaries for jobs of this type may range from $18,000 for an entry-level position to $50,000 for senior-level positions (all salaries quoted here are in Canadian dollars).

Jobs related to programming can be found in a wide range of agencies, with positions like recreation programmers, program coordinators, recreation technicians, camp co-coordinators or program leaders, and instructors in recreation and sport. These types of positions involve planning, organizing, supervising, and directing sport, social, cultural, youth, camp, special needs, and other recreational programs. Other responsibilities might include staff and instructors who supervise, prepare budgets, promote programs, assist community organizations or other clubs with special events, plan events, and so forth. These positions are a good starting point for entering the field, and the salaries range from $18,000 to $32,000.

Program leaders and instructors in recreation and sports are responsible for leading and instructing groups and individuals in recreational, sports, fitness, and athletic programs. Jobs might be found as aerobics instructors, camp counselors, day camp leaders, fitness instructors, playground workers, and so on. These occupations involve the ability to plan and carry out recreational activities and to understand the social and recreational needs of the community. Completion of secondary school and a college degree in recreation and physical education or extensive experience in a specific recreational or sports program are required. These types of positions and specific areas require certification also, such as a swimming or ski instructor's certificate or a first aid or fitness leadership certificate.

A variety of jobs might be found in therapeutic settings, long-term health care facilities, local community agencies, private and social services agencies, and schools. Therapeutic recreation professionals prepare leisure opportunities for persons with physical and developmental disabilities, older adults, youth at risk, and those living with mental health challenges.

Some of the titles related to this area are: clinical occupational therapist, community occupational therapist, recreational therapist, recreation consultant-special needs, occupational therapist rehabilitation consultant, or occupational therapist case manager. Professionals are employed as occupational therapists to develop individual and group programs for people affected by illness, developmental disorders, emotional or psychological problems, or aging. They work to help maintain, restore, or increase a consumer's ability to care for him or herself and to engage in work, school, or leisure. They also develop and implement health promotions programs with individuals, community groups, and employers. They have to analyze clients' capabilities and expectations related to life activities through observation, interview, and formal assessments, and then plan treatment programs.

A university degree in occupational therapy is required for this position; graduation from an occupational therapy program approved by the World Federation of Occupational Therapists (WFOT) is accepted in some provinces. Completion of the national certification examination may be required. Licensure with a regulatory body is required in all provinces except British Columbia, and membership in the national association, the Canadian Association of Occupational Therapists, is required in some provinces. Occupational therapists may obtain expertise in a particular area through additional training or experience.

Research and planning positions require involvement in developing and carrying out community studies, surveys, and environmental studies. Usually these positions require a four-year degree, or a higher level of education and experience in the field is necessary. Salaries for these types of jobs range from $25,000 to more than $50,000.

One type of research position is that of a recreation consultant. Duties include conducting research and developing programs and policies related to recreation. Occupations in this group are characterized by the general ability to advise and consult communities, corporations, institutions, and other organizations on the design and development of recreational programs and activities.

Recreation consultants need a university degree in recreation administration, sports administration, physical education, kinesiology, or a related discipline combined with some work experience in the recreation, sports, or fitness fields. Federal agencies, municipal and provincial governments, community centers, recreational institutions, and health and sports organizations are the employers that usually hire recreation consultants.

Jobs related to facility and park management are another important category for employment. Some examples of job titles include facility manager, supervisor, and park superintendent. The main responsibility for these kinds of positions is related to ensuring the safety of facility and staff. Salaries made by facility managers range from $18,000 to $50,000.

Park superintendents are responsible for developing and operating facilities, preparing budgets, planning for park areas, and supervising staff. Salaries for these positions range from $30,000 to $50,000 annually and typically require several years of experience.

The Canada Census data show that the average employment income for jobs in recreation, leisure, and related areas was $39,502 in 2000. Managers in art, culture, recreation, and sports earned on average $42,513, and recreation and sports program and service directors made $33,331.

Contacts on the Inside

Different associations and organizations in Canada offer informational and logistical support for recreation professionals. Often these groups provide a basis of networking and employment opportunities. The following are some national and regional associations and organizations that are closely related to recreation and parks:

Active Living Alliance for Canadians with a Disability (ALA)
720 Belfast Rd., Ste. 104
Ottawa, ON K1G 0Z5
www.ala.ca

Alberta Centre for Active Living
11759 Groat Rd.
Edmonton, AL T5M 3K6
www.centre4activeliving.ca

Alberta Recreation and Parks Association
11759 Groat Rd.
Percy Page Centre
Edmonton, AL T5M 3K6

Association Québécoise du Loisir Municipal
4545, Ave. Pierre-de-Coubertin
CP 1000, SUCC M
Montréal, QC H1V 3R2

Association des Travailleurs et Travalleuses
En Loisir du Nouveau-Brunswick Inc.
421 Ave. Acadie
Dieppe, NB E1A 1H4

Boys and Girls Clubs of Canada
7100 Woodbine Ave., Ste. 405
Markham, ON L3R 5J2
www.bgccan.com

British Columbia Recreation and Parks Association
30-10551 Shellbridge Way
Richmond, BC V6X 2W9

Canadian Association for the Advancement of Women and Sport
  and Physical Activity (CAAWS)
N202-801 King Edward Ave.
Ottawa, ON K1N 6N5
www.caaws.ca

Canadian Association for Health, Physical Education, Recreation,
  and Dance (CAHPERD)
2197 Riverside Dr., Ste. 403
Ottawa, ON K1H 7X3
www.cahperd.ca

Canadian Association for Leisure Studies (CALS)
www.eas.ualberta.ca/elj/cals/home.htm

Canadian Fitness and Lifestyle Research Institute (CFLRI)
201-185 Somerset St. West
Ottawa, ON K2P 0J2
www.cflri.ca

Canadian Institute of Child Health
384 Bank Street, Ste. 30
Ottawa, ON K2P 1Y4
www.cich.ca

Canadian Parks and Recreation Association
404-2197 Riverside Dr.
Ottawa, ON K1H 7X3
www.cpra.ca

Go for Green
5480 Canotek Rd., Unit #16
Gloucester, ON K1J 9H6
www.goforgreen.ca

National Fitness Leadership Advisory Council (NFLAC)
1600 James Naismith Dr., Ste. 306
Gloucester, ON K1B 5N4
www.magma.ca/~nflac

Newfoundland/Labrador Parks and Recreation Association
P.O. Box 8700
St. John's, NF A1B 4J6

Northwest Territories Recreation and Parks Association
P.O. Box 841
Yellowknife, NT X1A 2N6

Parks and Recreation Ontario
406-1185 Eglinton East
North York, ON M3C 3C6

Physical Activity Unit
Health Canada
Address Locator 1907C1
Tunney's Pasture
Ottawa, ON K1A 1B4
www.phac-aspc.gc.ca

Prince Edward Island Recreation and Facilities Association
109 Water St.
P.O. Box 1361
Summerside, PE C1N 4K2

Recreation Connections Manitoba
200 Main St.
Winnipeg, MB R3C 4M2

Recreation Nova Scotia
P.O. Box 3010 South
Halifax, NS B3J 3G6

Recreation and Parks Association of New Brunswick, Inc.
440 Wilsey Rd., Ste. 105
Fredericton, NB E3B 7G5
www.rpanb.nb.ca

Recreation and Parks Association of the Yukon
4061 Fourth Ave.
Whitehorse, YT Y1A 1H1

Saskatchewan Parks and Recreation Association
The Parkway Building
3303 Hillsdale Ave.
Regina, SK S4S 6W9

Colleges and Universities That Offer Curricula Related to Recreation and Leisure

For the following schools, the program and department name, the location, and the degrees offered—if available—are included.

United States

The schools listed here are arranged alphabetically by state.

Alabama

Alabama State University
Health, Physical Education, and Recreation
Montgomery, AL
B.A.
www.alasu.edu

Auburn University
Recreation Administration Program Area
Auburn, AL
B.A.
www.auburn.edu

Jacksonville State University
Health, Physical Education,
and Recreation
Jacksonville, AL
B.S.
www.jsu.edu

University of South Alabama
Leisure Studies
Mobile, AL
B.S. in Leisure Studies
M.S. in Recreation
Administration
M.S. in Therapeutic
Recreation
www.southalabama.edu

Alaska

Alaska Pacific University
Outdoor Studies Program
Anchorage, AK
B.S.
www.alaskapacific.edu

University of Alaska
Natural Resources
Management
Fairbanks, AK
B.S.
www.uaf.edu

Arizona

Arizona State University
Department of Recreation
Management and Tourism
Tempe, AZ
B.S., M.S.
www.asu.edu

Arizona State University, West
Department of Recreation and
Tourism Management
Phoenix, AZ
B.S.
www.west.asu.edu

Northern Arizona University
Parks and Recreation
Management
Flagstaff, AZ
B.A., B.S.
www.nau.edu

Arkansas

Arkansas Tech University
Parks, Recreation, and
Hospitality Administration
Russellville, AR
B.A.
www.atu.edu

Henderson State University
Recreation Division, HPER
Arkadelphia, AR
B.A.
www.hsu.edu

Southern Arkansas University
Department of Health,
Kinesiology, and
Recreation
Magnolia, AR
B.A.
www.saumag.edu

**University of Arkansas,
Fayetteville**
Department of Health
Science, Kinesiology,
Recreation, and Dance
Fayetteville, AR
B.S., M.A.T., M.Ed., M.S.,
Ed.D., Ph.D.
www.uark.edu

**University of Arkansas,
Pine Bluff**
Department of HPER
Pine Bluff, AR
B.A., M.A., Ph.D.
www.uapb.edu

California

**California Polytechnic State
University, San Luis Obispo**
Natural Resources
Management Department
San Luis Obispo, CA
B.S.
www.calpoly.edu

**California State University,
Chico**
Department of Recreation and
Parks Management
Chico, CA
www.csuchico.edu

**California State University,
Dominguez Hills**
Recreation and Leisure
Studies, PERD
Carson, CA
B.S., M.A. in Recreation
Administration
www.csudh.edu

California State University, Fresno

Recreation Administration
and Leisure Studies
Program
Fresno, CA
B.S.
www.csufresno.edu

California State University, Hayward

Department of Recreation and
Community Services
Hayward, CA
B.S.
www.csuhayward.edu

California State University, Long Beach

Department of Recreation and
Leisure Studies
Long Beach, CA
B.S. in Recreation
M.S. in Recreation
Administration
www.csulb.edu

California State University, Northridge

Department of Leisure Studies
and Recreation
Northridge, CA
B.S. in Recreation
B.S. in Recreation,
Therapeutic Recreation
Option
M.S. in Recreation
Administration
www.csun.edu

California State University, Sacramento

Department of Recreation and
Leisure Studies
Sacramento, CA
Minor, Certificate, B.S., M.S.
www.csus.edu

Humboldt State University

Recreation Administration
Program
Arcata, CA
B.A.
www.humboldt.edu

Los Medanos College
Travel Marketing
Pittsburg, CA
Associates
www.losmedanos.edu

Pepperdine, Seaver College
Leisure Science
Malibu, CA
B.A.
www.pepperdine.edu

San Diego State University
Department of Recreation
San Diego, CA
B.S. in Recreation
Administration with
emphasis in:
Recreation, Therapy
Recreation, Systems
Management, and Outdoor
Recreation
www.sdsu.edu

San Francisco State University
Department of Recreation and
Leisure Studies
San Francisco, CA
B.A., B.S., M.S.
www.sfsu.edu

San Jose State University
Department of Recreation and
Leisure Studies
San Jose, California
B.S., M.S.
www.sjsu.edu

Southwestern College
Recreation Education
Chula Vista, CA
www.swc.cc.ca.us

University of California, Davis
Environmental Planning and
Management
Davis, CA
B.A.
www.ucdavis.edu

University of California, Los Angeles
Physical Education
Department
Los Angeles, CA
B.A., M.A., Ph.D.
www.ucla.edu

University of LaVerne
Facilities Management
LaVerne, CA
B.A.
www.ulv.edu

Ventura College
Parks and Recreation
Management
Ventura, CA
B.A., M.A.
www.venturacollege.edu

Whittier College
Department of Recreation and
Physical Education
Whittier, CA
www.whittier.edu

Colorado

Adams State College
Health, Physical Education,
and Recreation
Department
Alamoca, CO
B.A., M.A.
www.adams.edu

**Colorado Mountain College,
Timberline**
Outdoor Recreation
Leadville, CO
A.G.S. (Associate in Graduate
Studies)
www.coloradomtn.edu

Colorado State University
Department of Natural
Resource Recreation and
Tourism
Fort Collins, CO
B.S., M.S., Ph.D.
www.colostate.edu

**Colorado State University,
Pueblo**
Exercise, Health Promotion,
and Recreation
Pueblo, CO
B.S.
www.colostate-pueblo.edu

Mesa State College
Department of Physical
Education, Recreation, and
Leisure
Grand Junction, CO
B.A.
www.mesastate.edu

**Metropolitan State College,
Denver**
Department of Human
Performance, Sport, and
Leisure
Denver, CO
B.A.
www.mscd.edu

University of Colorado, Boulder
>Tourism and Recreation
>Boulder, CO
>B.A., M.A.
>www.colorado.edu

University of Denver
>School of Hotel, Restaurant, and Tourism Management
>Denver, CO
>B.A.
>www.du.edu

University of Northern Colorado
>Recreation Program, Department of Human Services
>Greeley, CO
>B.S.
>www.unco.edu

Western State College of Colorado
>Kinesiology and Recreation Department
>Gunnison, CO
>B.A.
>www.western.edu

Connecticut

Eastern Connecticut State University
>Department of Physical Education and Recreation
>Willimantic, CT
>B.A.
>www.easternct.edu

Mitchell College
>Department of Physical Education, Recreation, and Fitness
>New London, CT
>A.S. in Therapeutic Recreation
>www.mitchell.edu

Southern Connecticut State University
>Department of Recreation and Leisure Studies
>New Haven, CT
>B.A., M.A.
>www.southernct.edu

University of Connecticut
Department of Sport Leisure
and Exercise Sciences
Storrs, CT
B.S., M.A., Sixth-Year
Diploma, and Ph.D.
www.uconn.edu

Delaware

Delaware State University
Park Management and
Recreation, HHP
Dover, DE
B.A.
www.desu.edu

University of Delaware
Recreation Department
Newark, DE
B.A.
www.udel.edu

District of Columbia

Gallaudet University
Recreation and Leisure
Studies Program
PER Department
Washington, DC
B.S.
www.gallaudet.edu

George Washington University
Kinetics and Leisure Studies
Washington, DC
B.A.
www.gwu.edu

Howard University
Physical Education and
Recreation Department
Washington, DC
B.A., M.A.
www.howard.edu

**University of the District of
Columbia**
Health, Physical Education,
and Leisure Studies
Washington, DC
B.A., M.A.
www.udc.edu

Florida

Eckerd College
Human Resources/Leisure
Services
St. Petersburg, FL
B.A.
www.eckerd.edu

Florida A&M University
Health, Physical Education,
and Recreation
Department
Tallahassee, FL
B.S.
www.famu.edu

Florida International University
Park and Recreation
Management
Miami, FL
B.A., M.A.
www.fiu.edu

Florida State University
Leisure Services and Studies
Tallahassee, FL
B.S., M.S.
www.fsu.edu

North Florida University
Health, Physical Education,
and Recreation
Department
Jacksonville, FL
B.A., M.A.
www.unf.edu

University of Central Florida
Department of Hospitality
Orlando, FL
B.A.
www.ucf.edu

University of Florida
Department of Recreation,
Parks, and Tourism
Gainesville, FL
B.S., M.S., Ph.D.
www.ufl.edu

University of Miami
Physical Therapy, Exercise
Science, Sport Studies
Coral Gables, FL
B.A., M.A.
www.miami.edu

University of West Florida
Health and Leisure Services
Department
Pensacola, FL
B.A., M.A.
www.uwf.edu

Warner Southern College
Department Physical
Education
Lake Wales, FL
B.S.
www.warner.edu

Georgia

Andrew College
Sports Management and
  Outdoor Leadership
Cuthbert, GA
Associates, Certificate
www.andrewcollege.edu

Atlanta Metropolitan College
Recreation Leadership
Atlanta, GA
Associates
www.atlm.edu

Columbus State University
Recreation and Park
  Administration Program,
  PELM
Columbus, GA
Associates, B.A.
www.colstate.edu

East Georgia College
Recreation Program
Statesboro, GA
Associates
www.ega.edu

Georgia Southern University
Department of Recreation and
  Leisure Services
Statesboro, GA
B.S. in Recreation
B.S. in Sport Management
M.A. in Recreation
  Administration
M.S. in Sport Management
www.georgiasouthern.edu

Georgia State University
Recreation and Leisure
  Studies, Department
  Kinesiology and Health
Atlanta, GA
B.A., M.A.
www.gsu.edu

Middle Georgia College
Recreation and Leisure
Cochran, GA
B.S.
www.mgc.edu

North Georgia College
Recreation Curriculum,
  HPER
Dahlonega, GA
B.A.
www.ngcsu.edu

Shorter College
Recreation Management
Program
Rome, GA
B.A.
www.shorter.edu

University of Georgia
Department of Recreation and
Leisure Studies
Athens, GA
B.S., M.Ed., M.A., Ed.D.
www.uga.edu

University of West Georgia
Recreation
Carrollton, GA
B.S.
www.westga.edu

Hawaii

University of Hawaii
Recreation and Leisure
Science Program
Honolulu, HI
B.A., M.A.
www.hawaii.edu

Idaho

**Brigham Young University,
Idaho**
Recreation Leadership
Rexburg, ID
B.S.
www.byui.edu

Northwest Nazarene University
Recreation and Leisure
Studies
Nampa, ID
B.A.
www.nnu.edu

University of Idaho
Department of Recreation,
College of Education
Moscow, ID
B.S. in Recreation
M.S. in Sport and Recreation
Management
www.uidaho.edu

University of Idaho
Department of Resource
Recreation and Tourism,
College of Natural
Resources
Moscow, ID
B.S., M.S., Ph.D.
www.uidaho.edu

Illinois

Aurora University
Recreation Administration
Department
Aurora, IL
B.S., M.S.
www.aurora.edu

Chicago State University
Health, Physical Education,
and Recreation
Department
Chicago, IL
B.A., M.A.
www.csu.edu

Eastern Illinois University
Department of Leisure Studies
Charleston, IL
B.S.
www.eiu.edu

Elmhurst College
Health, Physical Education,
and Recreation
Department
Elmhurst, IL
B.A.
www.elmhurst.edu

Illinois State University
Recreation and Park
Administration Program
Normal, IL
B.S. in Recreation and Park
Administration
M.S. in Health, Physical
Education, and Recreation
www.ilstu.edu

Kennedy-King College
Recreation Program
Chicago, IL
B.A.
www.kennedyking.ccc.edu

McKendree College
Parks and Recreation
Lebanon, IL
B.A.
www.mckendree.edu

Northeastern Illinois University
Department of Health,
Physical Education, and
Recreation Administration
Chicago, IL
B.A.
www.neiu.edu

Southern Illinois University
Department of Health
Education, Education, and
Recreation
Carbondale, IL
B.S. in Education (Recreation)
M.S. in Education
(Recreation)
www.siu.edu

University of Illinois
Department of Leisure Studies
Champaign, IL
B.S., M.S., Ph.D. with
specialization in Leisure
Studies
www.uiuc.edu

University of St. Francis
Department of Recreation
Administration
Joliet, IL
B.A.
www.stfrancis.edu

Western Illinois University
Department of Recreation,
Park, and Tourism
Administration
Macomb, IL
B.S., M.Ed.
www.wiu.edu

Indiana

Anderson University
Physical Education Program
in Recreation Leadership
Anderson, IN
B.A.
www.anderson.edu

Ball State University
Office of Recreation Programs
Muncie, IN
B.A., M.A.
www.bsu.edu

Huntington University
Recreation Management
Huntington, IN
B.A.
www.huntington.edu

Indiana State University
Department of Recreation and
Sport Management
Terre Haute, IN
B.A, B.S., M.S.
www.indstate.edu

Indiana University
Department of Recreation and
Park Administration
Bloomington, IN
B.S., M.S., Re.Dir., Re.D.,
Ph.D.
www.indiana.edu

Purdue University
Physical Education, Health,
and Recreation Services
Department
West Lafayette, IN
B.A., M.A., Ph.D.
www.purdue.edu

Taylor University
Health, Physical Education,
and Recreation
Department
Upland, IN
B.A.
www.taylor.edu

Vincennes University
Recreation Management
Vincennes, IN
B.S.
www.vinu.edu

Iowa

Drake University
Recreation and Leisure
Department
Des Moines, IA
B.A., M.A.
www.drake.edu

Graceland University
Recreation Program
Lamoni, IA
B.A.
www.graceland.edu

Iowa State University
Leisure Studies
Ames, IA
B.A.
www.iastate.edu

Morningside College
Department of Health,
Physical Education, and
Recreation
Sioux City, IA
B.A.
www.morningside.edu

Northwestern College
Recreation Department
Orange City, IA
B.A.
www.nwc.edu

University of Iowa
Department of Sport, Health,
Leisure, and Physical
Studies
Iowa City, IA
B.S., M.A.
www.uiowa.edu

University of Northern Iowa
Leisure Services Division
Cedar Falls, IA
B.A. with options in
Programming and
Therapeutic Recreation
M.A. with options in Leisure
Services, Youth/Human
Service, Agency
Administration
www.uni.edu

Upper Iowa University
Department Health, Physical
Education, and Recreation
Fayette, IA
B.A.
www.uiu.edu

Wartburg College
Leisure Services
Waverly, IA
B.A.
www.wartburg.edu

Kansas

Kansas State University
Recreation Resources Division
Manhattan, KS
B.S.
www.ksu.edu

Mid-America Nazarene College
Department of Health,
Physical Education, and
Recreation
Olathe, KS
B.A.
www.manc.edu

Pittsburg State University
Health, Physical Education,
and Recreation
Department
Pittsburg, KS
B.A., M.A.
www.pittstate.edu

University of Kansas
Department of Health,
Physical Education, and
Recreation
Lawrence, KS
B.A., M.A.
www.ku.edu

Wichita State University
Department of Health,
Physical Education, and
Recreation
Wichita, KS
B.A.
www.wichita.edu

Kentucky

Asbury College
Department of Recreation
Wilmore, KY
B.A.
www.asbury.edu

Cumberland College
Department of Recreation
Williamsburg, KY
B.A.
www.cumberlandcollege.edu

Eastern Kentucky University
Department of Leisure Studies
Richmond, KY
B.S., M.S.
www.eku.edu

Georgetown College
Recreation Program
Georgetown, KY
B.A.
www.georgetowncollege.edu

Morehead State University
Physical Education and
Recreation
Morehead, KY
B.A.
www.morehead-st.edu

Murray State University
Health, Physical Education,
and Recreation
Department
Murray, KY
B.A., M.A.
www.murraystate.edu

University of Kentucky
Recreation and Leisure
Studies
Lexington, KY
B.A., M.A.
www.uky.edu

University of Louisville
Physical Education and
Recreation
Louisville, KY
B.A.
www.louisville.edu

Western Kentucky University
Recreation and Park
Administration
Bowling Green, KY
B.S., M.S.
www.wku.edu

Louisiana

Grambling State University
Recreation Careers Program
Grambling, LA
B.S. in Leisure Studies with
emphasis in Therapeutic
Recreation and Recreation
Program Service Delivery
www.gram.edu

**Southern University and A&M
College**
Department of Leisure and
Recreation Services
Baton Rouge, LA
B.A., M.A.
www.subr.edu

**Southern University, New
Orleans**
New Orleans, LA
B.A.
www.suno.edu

University of Louisiana
Health and Physical
Education Department
Lafayette, LA
B.A.
www.louisiana.edu

Maine

Unity College
Programs in Outdoor
Recreation, Environmental
Education, and Park
Management
Unity, ME
B.A.
www.unity.edu

University of Maine, Machias
Program in Recreation
Management
Machias, ME
Associates, B.A.
www.umm.maine.edu

University of Maine, Orono
Forest Management
Orono, ME
B.S.
www.umaine.edu

University of Maine,
Presque Isle
Department of Recreation and
Leisure Services
Presque Isle, ME
Minor, Associates, B.S. with
an option for Park Law
Enforcement emphasis
www.umpi.maine.edu

University of New England
Sports and Fitness
Management
Biddeford, ME
B.S.
www.une.edu

University of Southern Maine
Recreation and Leisure
Studies
Portland, ME
B.S.
www.usm.maine.edu

Maryland

Frostburg State University
Recreation Program
Frostburg, MD
B.S., M.S.
www.frostburg.edu

Mid-State College
Travel and Tourism
Peoria, MD
Associates
www.midstate.edu

Morgan State University
Hospitality Management
Baltimore, MD
B.A.
www.morgan.edu

University of Baltimore
Recreation and Leisure
Studies
Baltimore, MD
B.A., M.A.
www.ubalt.edu

University of Maryland
Natural Resource
Management
College Park, MD
B.S.
www.umd.edu

Massachusetts

Boston University
Leisure Studies
Boston, MA
Ed.M.
www.bu.edu

Gordon College
Department of Recreation and
Leisure Studies
Wenham, MA
B.A.
www.gordon.edu

Northeastern University
Health, Sport, and Leisure
Studies
Boston, MA
B.A., M.A.
www.northeastern.edu

Springfield College
Department of Recreation and
Leisure Services
Springfield, MA
B.S. degrees in Therapeutic
Recreation, Recreation
Management, and Outdoor
Recreation Management
M.Ed. and M.S. degrees in
Therapeutic Recreation
Management, Recreation
Management, and Outdoor
Recreation Management
www.spfldcol.edu

**University of Massachusetts,
Amherst**
Leisure Studies and Resources
Amherst, MA
Associates, B.A.
www.umass.edu

Michigan

Baker College
Center for Graduate Studies
(multiple locations)
M.A.
www.baker.edu

Central Michigan University
Department of Recreation,
Parks, and Leisure Services
Administration
Mt. Pleasant, MI
B.A., B.A.A., B.S., M.A.,
M.S.
www.cmich.edu

Eastern Michigan University
Recreation and Parks
Ypsilanti, MI
B.A.
www.emich.edu

Ferris State University
Recreation Leadership and
    Management
Big Rapids, MI
B.A.
www.ferris.edu

Grand Valley State University
Therapeutic Recreation
    Program
Allendale, MI
B.S.
www.gvsu.edu

Lake Superior State University
Recreation Studies and
    Exercise Science
Sault Ste. Marie, MI
B.A.
www.lssu.edu

Michigan State University
Department of Park,
    Recreation, and Tourism
    Resources
East Lansing, MI
B.S., M.S., Ph.D.
www.msu.edu

Northern Michigan University
Department of Health,
    Physical Education, and
    Recreation
Marquette, MI
B.A., M.A.
www.nmu.edu

University of Michigan
Natural Resources and
    Environment
Ann Arbor, MI
B.A., M.A., Ph.D.
www.umich.edu

Wayne State University
Interdisciplinary Studies with
    post-B.A. certificate or
    minor in Nonprofit Sector
Detroit, MI
www.wayne.edu

Western Michigan University
Department of Health,
    Physical Education, and
    Recreation
Kalamazoo, MI
Minor, B.S. (Nonteaching)
www.wmich.edu

Minnesota

Bemidji State University

Health, Physical Education,
and Recreation
Department
Bemidji, MN
B.A.
www.bemidjistate.edu

Minnesota State University, Mankato

Department of Recreation,
Parks, and Leisure Services
Mankato, MN
B.S. in Recreation, Parks, and
Leisure Services
M.S. in Multidisciplinary
Recreation
www.mnsu.edu

St. Cloud University

Recreation Administration
St. Cloud, MN
B.A.
www.stcloudstate.edu

University of Minnesota

Division of Recreation, Park,
and Leisure Studies
Minneapolis, MN
B.S., M.Ed., M.A. in
Recreation, Park, and
Leisure Studies
Ph.D. in Education and
Human Development
(emphasis in Recreation,
Park, and Leisure Studies)
www.umn.edu

University of Minnesota, Crookston

Park and Recreation Resource
Management
Crookston, MN
B.A.
www.crk.umn.edu

University of Minnesota, Duluth

Health, Physical Education,
and Recreation
Department
Duluth, MN
B.A.
www.d.umn.edu

Winona State University
   Recreation and Leisure
      Studies
   Winona, MN
   B.A., M.A.
   www.winona.edu

Mississippi

Alcorn State University
   Health, Physical Education,
      and Recreation
      Department
   Alcorn State, MS
   B.A.
   www.alcorn.edu

Jackson State University
   Health, Physical Education,
      and Recreation
      Department
   Jackson, MS
   B.A.
   www.jsums.edu

University of Mississippi
   Department of Exercise
      Science and Leisure
      Management
   University, MS
   B.A., M.A., Ph.D.
   www.olemiss.edu

**University of Southern
Mississippi**
   Recreation Program, School of
      Human Performance and
      Recreation
   Hattiesburg, MS
   B.S., M.S.
   www.usm.edu

Missouri

**Central Missouri State
University**
   Recreation and Tourism
   Warrensburg, MO
   B.A., M.A.
   www.cmsu.edu

Missouri Western State College
   Health, Physical Education,
      and Recreation
   St. Joseph, MO
   B.A.
   www.mwsc.edu

**Northwest Missouri State
University**
   Department of Health,
      Physical Education, and
      Recreation
   Maryville, MO
   B.S., M.S.Ed.
   www.nwmissouri.edu

Southeast Missouri State University
Department of Health and Leisure
Cape Girardeau, MO
B.S.
www.semo.edu

Southwest Baptist University
Recreation Department
Bolivar, MO
B.A.
www.sbuniv.edu

Southwest Missouri State University
Recreation and Leisure Studies
Springfield, MO
B.S.
www.smsu.edu

University of Missouri
Department of Parks, Recreation, and Tourism
Columbia, MO
B.S., M.S.
www.missouri.edu

Montana

Montana State University
Division of Health, Nutrition, and Movement Science
Bozeman, MT
B.A.
www.montana.edu

University of Montana
Recreation Management Program
Missoula, MT
B.S., M.S., Ph.D.
www.umt.edu

Nebraska

College of St. Mary
Health, Physical Education, and Recreation Department
Omaha, NE
Associates, B.A.
www.csm.edu

Nebraska Wesleyan University
Health and Human Performance Department
Lincoln, NE
B.A.
www.nebrwesleyan.edu

University of Nebraska, Kearney
Recreation and Leisure
Studies
Kearney, NE
B.A.
www.unk.edu

University of Nebraska, Lincoln
Recreation and Leisure
Studies
Lincoln, NE
B.A.
www.unl.edu

University of Nebraska, Omaha
Recreation and Leisure
Studies
Omaha, NE
B.S., M.A., M.S.
www.unomaha.edu

Nevada

University of Nevada, Las Vegas
Leisure Studies, Department
of Tourism and
Conventions
Las Vegas, NV
B.S., M.S.
www.unlv.edu

University of Nevada, Reno
Health Ecology
Reno, NV
B.A.
www.unr.edu

New Hampshire

Franklin Pierce College
Recreation Management
Program
Rindge, NH
B.A.
www.fpc.edu

Plymouth State College
Environmental Planning
Plymouth, NH
B.S.
www.plymouth.edu

University of New Hampshire
Department of Recreation
Management and Policy
Durham, NH
B.S., M.A.
www.unh.edu

New Jersey

Essex County College
Physical Education Program
Newark, NJ
A.S.
www.essex.edu

Kean University
Recreation Administration
Union, NJ
B.A.
www.kean.edu

Montclair State University
Health Professions, Physical
Education, Recreation,
and Leisure Studies
Upper Montclair, NJ
B.A.
www.montclair.edu

New Jersey City University
Department of Sports and
Leisure
Jersey City, NJ
B.A.
www.njcu.edu

Rutgers University
Recreation and Leisure
Studies
New Brunswick, NJ
B.A.
www.rutgers.edu

Thomas Edison State College
Parks and Recreation Program
Trenton, NJ
B.S., Associates
www.tesc.edu

**William Paterson University of
New Jersey**
Movement Science and
Leisure Studies
Wayne, NJ
B.A.
www.wpunj.edu

New Mexico

**New Mexico Highlands
University**
Tourism, Leisure, and Sports
Management
Las Vegas, NM
Associates, B.A.
www.nmhu.edu

New Mexico State University
Recreational Area
Management
Las Cruces, NM
B.S.
www.nmsu.edu

University of New Mexico
Department of Health,
Physical Education, and
Recreation
Albuquerque, NM
B.A., M.A., Ph.D.
www.unm.edu

New York

Ithaca College
Department of Therapeutic
Recreation and Leisure
Services
Ithaca, NY
B.S.
www.ithaca.edu

Lehman College, CUNY
Leisure Sciences Program
Bronx, NY
www.lehman.cuny.edu

Medaille College
Recreation and Parks
Management
Buffalo, NY
B.A., M.A.
www.medaille.edu

Mercy College
Therapeutic Recreation
Dobbs Ferry, NY
B.A.
www.mercy.edu

Niagara University
Institute of Travel, Hotel, and
Restaurant Administration
Niagara University, NY
B.A.
www.niagara.edu

St. Joseph's College
Recreation Department
Patchog, NY
B.A., M.A.
www.sjcny.edu

**State University of New York,
College at Brockport**
Recreation and Leisure
Studies Department
Brockport, NY
B.S., M.S.
www.brockport.edu

State University of New York, College at Cortland
Department of Recreation and
Leisure Studies
Cortland, NY
B.S., B.S.E., M.S., M.S.E.
www.cortland.edu

State University of New York, Syracuse
College of Environmental
Science and Forestry
Syracuse, NY
B.A.
www.esf.edu

Utica College of Syracuse
Therapeutic Recreation
Program
Syracuse, NY
B.A.
www.utica.edu

North Carolina

Appalachian State University
Leisure Studies Program
Boone, NC
B.S. in Recreation
Management
www.appstate.edu

Belmont Abbey College
Recreational Studies
Wheeler Center
Belmont, NC
B.A.
www.belmontabbeycollege.edu

Catawba College
Health, Physical Education,
and Recreation
Department
Salisbury, NC
B.A.
www.catawba.edu

East Carolina University
Department of Recreation and
Leisure Studies
Greenville, NC
B.S.
www.ecu.edu

Elon College
Leisure and Sport
Management
Elon College, NC
B.S.
www.elon.edu

Louisburg College
Health and Physical
Education
Louisburg, NC
A.S.
www.louisburg.edu

Mars Hill College
Recreation Department
Mars Hill, NC
B.A.
www.mhc.edu

Montreat Anderson College
Sport Management
Montreat, NC
B.S.
www.montreat.edu

Mount Olive College
Department of Recreation and
Leisure Studies
Mount Olive, NC
B.A., B.S.
www.mountolivecollege.edu

**North Carolina Agricultural
and Technical University**
Recreation Administration
Greensboro, NC
B.A.
www.ncat.edu

**North Carolina Central
University**
Parks and Recreation
Management
Durham, NC
B.A., M.A.
www.nccu.edu

North Carolina State University
Department of Parks,
Recreation, and Tourism
Management
Raleigh, NC
B.S., M.S., M.R.P.T.M., M.
Nat. Res.
www.ncsu.edu

**University of North Carolina,
Chapel Hill**
Leisure Studies and
Recreation Administration
Chapel Hill, NC
B.A. in Recreation
Administration
M.S. in Recreation
Administration (M.S.R.A.)
www.unc.edu

University of North Carolina, Greensboro

   Department of Recreation,
      Parks, and Tourism
   Greensboro, NC
   B.S., M.S.
   www.uncg.edu

University of North Carolina, Pembroke

   Department of Leisure Studies
   Pembroke, NC
   B.S., M.S.
   www.uncp.edu

University of North Carolina, Wilmington

   Department of Health,
      Physical Education, and
      Recreation
   Wilmington, NC
   B.A. in Parks and Recreation
      Management
   www.uncw.edu

Warren Wilson College

   Outdoor Leadership Studies
   Asheville, NC
   B.A.
   www.warren-wilson.edu

Western Carolina University

   Parks and Recreation
      Management Program
   Cullowhee, NC
   B.S.
   www.wcu.edu

Wingate College

   Parks and Recreation
      Administration Program
   Wingate, NC
   Associates, B.A.
   www.wingate.edu

Winston-Salem State University

   Therapeutic Recreation
      Program
   Winston-Salem, NC
   B.A.
   www.wssu.edu

North Dakota

Minot State University, Bottineau

   Parks and Recreation Program
   Bottineau, ND
   A.A.S. in Parks and
      Recreation Technology
   A.S. in Park Management
   www.misu-b.nodak.edu

North Dakota State University, Fargo
Natural Resource Management
Fargo, ND
B.A., M.A.
www.ndsu.nodak.edu

University of North Dakota
Recreation and Leisure
Services Program
Grand Forks, ND
B.S.
www.und.edu

Ohio

Ashland University
Department of Sport Sciences
Ashland, OH
B.S. in Recreation
Administration
B.S. in Therapeutic
Recreation
www.ashland.edu

Bowling Green State University
Sport Management,
Recreation, and Tourism
Division
Bowling Green, OH
B.S. in Education
M.S. in Education
www.bgsu.edu

Central State University
Recreation Program
Wilberforce, OH
B.A.
www.centralstate.edu

Kent State University
Leisure Studies
Kent, OH
B.S., M.A.
www.kent.edu

Miami University of Ohio
Physical Health Sciences
Miami, OH
B.A.
www.muohio.edu

Ohio State University
Parks, Recreation, and
Tourism Administration
Columbus, OH
B.A., M.A.
www.osu.edu

Ohio University
School of Recreation and
Sport Sciences
Athens, OH
B.S. in Recreation Studies
M.S. in Physical Education
with a concentration in
Recreation
www.ohiou.edu

Shawnee State College
Recreation and Parks
Management Program
Portsmouth, OH
B.A.
www.shawnee.edu

University of Findlay
Recreation Therapy Program
Findlay, OH
B.A.
www.findlay.edu

University of Toledo
Recreation and Leisure
Studies
Toledo, OH
B.Ed. with specialization in
Resource Management,
Law Enforcement,
Community
Special Recreation,
Community Recreation,
Therapeutic Recreation
M.Ed. with emphasis in
Recreation Administration
or Therapeutic Recreation
www.utoledo.edu

Oklahoma

**Eastern Oklahoma State
College**
Park/Nursery Management,
Forest Technology
Wilburton, OK
B.A.
www.eosc.edu

Langston University
Health, Physical Education,
and Recreation
Langston, OK
B.A.
www.lunet.edu

Oklahoma State University
Leisure Studies
Stillwater, OK
B.S. in Leisure Studies
M.S. in HPEL, emphasis in
Leisure Studies
Doctor of Education in
Applied Educational
Studies
Doctor of Philosophy in
Environmental Science
www.okstate.edu

Oral Roberts University
Health, Physical Education,
and Recreation
Department
Tulsa, OK
B.A.
www.oru.edu

**Southwestern Oklahoma State
University**
Health, Physical Education,
and Recreation
Weatherford, OK
B.A.
www.swosu.edu

**University of Central
Oklahoma**
Kinesiology and Health
Studies
Edmond, OK
B.A.
www.ucok.edu

University of Oklahoma
Health, Physical Education,
and Recreation
Department
Administration
Norman, OK
B.A., M.A.
www.uo.edu

University of Tulsa
Health, Physical Education,
and Recreation
Tulsa, OK
B.A., M.A.
www.utulsa.edu

Pennsylvania

**California University of
Pennsylvania**
Parks and Recreation
Management Program
California, PA
B.A.
www.cup.edu

Cheyney State University
Health, Physical Education,
and Recreation
Department
Cheyney, PA
B.A.
www.cheyney.edu

East Stroudsburg University
Department of Recreation and
Leisure Services
Management
East Stroudsburg, PA
B.S. in Recreation and Leisure
Services Management
www.esu.edu

Gannon University
  Recreation and Leisure
    Studies
  Erie, PA
  Associates, B.A.
  www.gannon.edu

Lebanon Valley College
  Travel Program
  Annville, PA
  B.A.
  www.lvc.edu

Lincoln University
  Department of Health,
    Physical Education, and
    Recreation
  Lincoln University, PA
  B.S. in Recreation with option
    in Therapeutic Recreation
  www.lincoln.edu

Lock Haven University
  Recreation Department
  Lock Haven, PA
  B.A.
  www.lhup.edu

Messiah College
  Health, Physical Education,
    and Recreation
    Department
  Grantham, PA
  B.A.
  www.messiah.edu

**Pennsylvania State University,
Abington College**
  Recreation Leadership
  University Park, PA
  B.S., M.S., M.Ed., and Ph.D.
  www.abington.psu.edu

Pennsylvania State University
  Recreation Leadership
  University Park, PA
  B.S., M.S., M.Ed., and Ph.D.
  www.psu.edu

Slippery Rock University
  Department of Parks and
    Recreation/Environmental
    Education
  Slippery Rock, PA
  B.S., M.S., M.Ed.
  www.sru.edu

Temple University
Department of Sport and
Recreation Management
Philadelphia, PA
B.S., M.Ed.
www.temple.edu

West Chester University
Leisure Studies and Dance
West Chester, PA
B.A.
www.wcupa.edu

York College
Recreation and Leisure
Administration
York, PA
B.S.
www.ycp.edu

Rhode Island

Rhode Island College
Recreation Program
Providence, RI
B.A.
www.ric.edu

South Carolina

Benedict College
Health, Physical
Education, and Recreation
Department
Columbia, SC
B.A.
www.benedict.edu

Claflin University
Department of Health and
Physical Education
Orangeburg, SC
B.A.
www.claflin.edu

Clemson University
Department of Parks,
Recreation, and Tourism
Management
Clemson, SC
B.S., M.P.R.T.M., M.S.,
Ph.D.
www.clemson.edu

North Greenville College
Park and Recreation Program
Tigerville, SC
B.A.
www.ngc.edu

Winthrop University
Department of Health and
Physical Education
Rock Hill, SC
B.A.
www.winthrop.edu

South Dakota

Black Hills State University
Tourism and Hospitality
Management
Spearfish, SD
B.A.
www.bhsu.edu

Northern State College
Recreation Curriculum
Aberdeen, SD
B.A.
www.northern.edu

South Dakota State University
Health, Physical Education,
and Recreation
Department
Brookings, SD
B.A.
www3.sdstate.edu

University of South Dakota
Division of Health, Physical
Education, and Recreation
Vermillion, SD
B.A.
www.usd.edu

Tennessee

Austin Peay State University
Parks and Recreation Program
Clarksville, TN
B.A.
www.apsu.edu

Belmont University
Park and Recreation Program
Nashville, TN
B.A.
www.belmont.edu

Bethel College
Park and Recreation Program
McKenzie, TN
B.A.
www.bethel.edu

Carson-Newman College
Department of Health,
Physical Education, and
Leisure Services
Jefferson City, TN
B.A.
www.cn.edu

Cumberland University
Recreation Department
Lebanon, TN
B.A.
www.cumberland.edu

East Tennessee State University
Physical Education, Exercise,
and Sport Science
Department
Johnson City, TN
B.A.
www.etsu.edu

Fisk University
Recreation Department
Nashville, TN
B.A.
www.fisk.edu

Lambuth University
Recreation Department
Jackson, TN
B.A.
www.lambuth.edu

Middle Tennessee State University
Recreation Program
Murfreesboro, TN
B.S., M.S.
www.mtsu.edu

Tennessee Technical University
Recreation Department
Cookeville, TN
B.A.
www.tntech.edu

University of Memphis
Recreation, Park, and Leisure
Academic Department
Memphis, TN
B.A., M.A.
www.memphis.edu

University of Tennessee, Chattanooga
Department of Education,
Health, and Leisure
Services
Chattanooga, TN
B.A.
www.utc.edu

University of Tennessee, Knoxville
   Recreation and Tourism
      Management.
   Knoxville, TN
   B.S., M.S.
   www.utk.edu

University of Tennessee, Martin
   Park and Recreation
      Administration
   Martin, TN
   B.A.
   www.utm.edu

Texas

Alamo Community College District
   Recreation Leadership
      Program
   San Antonio, TX
   B.A.
   www.accd.edu

Baylor University
   Leisure Services Division
   Waco, TX
   B.A.
   www.baylor.edu

Stephen F. Austin State University
   Forest Recreation
   Nacogdoches, TX
   B.A.
   www.sfasu.edu

Texas A&M University
   Department of Recreation,
      Park, and Tourism Sciences
   College Station, TX
   B.S. in Recreation, Park, and
      Tourism Sciences
   M.S. and Ph.D. in
      Recreation, Park, and
      Tourism Sciences
   M.Agr. in Recreation and
      Resources Development
   M.Agr. in Natural Resources
      Development
   www.tamu.edu

Texas State University
   Division of Recreation
      Administration
   San Marcos, TX
   B.A.
   www.txstate.edu

Texas Technical University
Park Administration and
Landscape Architecture
Lubbock, TX
B.A., M.A.
www.ttu.edu

University of North Texas
Recreation and Leisure
Studies
Denton, TX
B.S., M.S. in Recreation and
Leisure Studies
www.unt.edu

Utah

Brigham Young University
Department of Recreation
Management and Youth
Leadership
Provo, UT
B.S. in Leisure Services
Management, Therapeutic
Recreation, and Youth
Leadership
M.S. in Recreation
Management
www.byu.edu

University of Utah
Department of Parks,
Recreation, and Tourism
Salt Lake City, UT
B.S., B.A., M.S., M. Phil.,
Ed.D., and Ph.D. in Parks,
Recreation, and Tourism
www.utah.edu

Utah State University
Department of Health,
Physical Education, and
Recreation
Logan, UT
B.S., M.A., Ph.D.
www.usu.edu

Utah State University
Forest Resources Department
Logan, UT
B.A., M.A., Ph.D.
www.usu.edu

Utah Valley State College
Hospitality Management and
Facilities Management
Orem, UT
A.A.S., A.S., B.S.
www.uvsc.edu

Vermont

Green Mountain College
Department of Recreation and
    Leisure Studies
Poultney, VT
B.S. in Therapeutic
    Recreation
B.S. in Recreation
B.S. in Leisure Resource
    Facilities Management
B.S. in Adventure Recreation
www.greenmtn.edu

Johnson State College
Business Management and
    Economics Department
Johnson, VT 05656
B.A.
www.johnsonstatecollege.edu

Lyndon State College
Department of Recreation
    Resource and Ski Resort
    Management
Lyndonville, VT
B.S.
www.lyndonstate.edu

Norwich University
Health, Physical Education,
    and Recreation
    Department
Northfield, VT
B.A.
www.norwich.edu

University of Vermont
Recreation Management
    Program
Burlington, VT
www.uvm.edu

Virginia

**Christopher Newport
University**
Recreation, Sports, Wellness
    Management
Newport News, VA
B.A.
www.cnu.edu

Eastern Mennonite University
Department of Physical
    Education and Recreation
Harrisonburg, VA
B.A.
www.emu.edu

Ferrum College
Recreation and Leisure
Program
Ferrum, VA
B.S. in Recreation and
Leisure—Generalists
B.S. in Outdoor Recreation
www.ferrum.edu

George Mason University
Health, Fitness, and
Recreation
Manassas, VA
B.S.
www.gmu.edu

Hampton University
Health, Physical Education,
and Recreation
Hampton, VA
B.A.
www.hamptonu.edu

James Madison University
Health Sciences Department
Harrisonburg, VA
B.A.
www.jmu.edu

Longwood College
Department of Health,
Physical Education,
Recreation, and Dance
Farmville, VA
B.S. in Therapeutic
Recreation
www.longwood.edu

Lynchburg College
Recreation Program
Lynchburg, VA
B.A.
www.lynchburg.edu

Marymount College of Virginia
Physical Fitness Management
Arlington, VA
Associates, B.A.
www.marymount.edu

Norfolk State University
Health, Physical Education,
and Exercise Science
Norfolk, VA
B.A.
www.nsu.edu

Old Dominion University
Recreation and Leisure
Studies Program
Norfolk, VA
B.S., M.S.
www.odu.edu

Radford University
Department of Leisure
Services
Radford, VA
B.S., B.A.
www.radford.edu

Shenandoah University
Department of Physical
Education and Recreation
Winchester, VA
B.A.
www.su.edu

Virginia Commonwealth University
Recreation, Parks, and
Tourism Program
Richmond, VA
B.S., M.S.
www.vcu.edu

Virginia Polytechnic Institute
Department of Forestry
Blacksburg, VA
B.A., M.A., Ph.D.
www.vt.edu

Virginia State University
Recreation Curriculum
Petersburg, VA
B.A.
www.vsu.edu

Virginia Union University
Department of Recreation
Richmond, VA
B.A.
www.vuu.edu

Washington

Centralia College
Health, Physical Education,
and Recreation
Department
Centralia, WA
B.A.
www.centralia.ctc.edu

Clark College
Recreation and Leisure
Vancouver, WA
B.A.
www.clark.edu

Eastern Washington University
Physical Education, Health,
and Recreation
Department
Cheney, WA
B.A. in Recreation and
Leisure Services
www.ewu.edu

Gonzaga University
Recreation, Parks, and Leisure
Spokane, WA
B.A.
www.gonzaga.edu

Pierce College
Recreation, Parks, and Leisure
Services
Lakewood, WA
B.A.
www.pierce.ctc.edu

Skagit Valley College
Recreation Technology
Mount Vernon, WA
B.A.
www.skagit.edu

University of Washington
Forest Resources
Seattle, WA
B.A.
www.washington.edu

Washington State University
Recreation Administration
and Leisure Studies
Pullman, WA
B.A., M.A.
www.wsu.edu

Washington State University
Wildlife Wildland Recreation
Management
Pullman, WA
B.A., M.A.
www.wsu.edu

Western Washington University
Recreation Program
Bellingham, WA
B.A.
www.wwu.edu

West Virginia

Alderson-Broaddus College
Recreation Leadership
Philippi, WV
B.A.
www.blue.ab.edu

Davis and Elkins College
Recreation Management and
Tourism Program
Elkins, WV
B.A.
www.davisandelkins.edu

Marshall University
Park Resources and Leisure
Services
Huntington, WV
B.S.
www.marshall.edu

Shepherd College
Recreation and Leisure
Services
Shepherdstown, WV
B.A.
www.shepherd.edu

West Virginia State College
Recreation Program,
Department of HPERS
Institute, WV
B.A.
www.wvsc.edu

West Virginia University
Recreation and Parks
Management
Morgantown, WV
B.S.R. in Recreation
M.S.R. in Recreation
www.wvu.edu

West Virginia Wesleyan College
Department of Recreation and
Leisure Studies
Buckhannon, WV
B.A.
www.wvwc.edu

Wisconsin

Bryant and Stratton College
Travel Hospitality
Management
Milwaukee, WI
B.A.
www.bryantstratton.edu

**University of Wisconsin,
La Crosse**
Exercise Science, Health, and
Recreation
LaCrosse, WI
B.S.
www.uwlax.edu

**University of Wisconsin,
Milwaukee**
Department of Human
Kinetics
Milwaukee, WI
B.S.
www.uwm.edu

**University of Wisconsin,
River Falls**
Scientific Land Management
Department of Health and
Human Performance
River Falls, WI
B.A.
www.uwrf.edu

Wyoming

Central Wyoming College
Recreation Leadership
Program
Riverton, WY
B.A.
www.cwc.edu

University of Wyoming
Department of Geography
and Recreation
Laramie, WY
B.S., M.S.
www.uwyo.edu

Canada

The schools listed here are arranged alphabetically by province.

Alberta

Augustana University
Recreation Administration
Camrose, AB
B.A.
www.augustana.ab.ca

Canadian Union College
Outward Pursuits
Lacombe, AB
Associates, B.A.
www.cauc.ca

Fairview College
Golf Course and Park
Management
Fairview, AB
B.A.
www.fairviewc.ab.ca

Grand Prairie Regional College
Recreation Administration
Grand Prairie, AB
Associates
www.gprc.ab.ca

Grant MacEwan Community College
Golf Operation Management
Edmonton, AB
Associates
www.macewan.ca

Lakeland College
Adventure Tourism and
  Outdoor Recreation,
  Tourism Management,
  Environmental Sciences
Vermilion, AB
B.A.
www.lakelandc.ab.ca

Lethbridge Community College
Recreation and Leisure
  Services Management
Lethbridge, AB
Associates
www.lethbridgecollege.ab.ca

Medicine Hat College
Recreation Administration
Medicine Hat, AB
B.A.
www.mhc.ab.ca

Mount Royal College
Leisure Services
Calgary, AB
B.A.
www.mtroyal.ab.ca

North Alberta Institute of Technology
Environmental Science,
  Landscape Architecture
Edmonton, AB
B.A.
www.nait.ab.ca

Red Deer College
Recreation Administration
Associates in Hospitality and
  Tourism
Red Deer, AB
B.A. in Recreation and
  Leisure Studies
www.rdc.ab.ca

Southern Alberta Institute of Technology
Recreation Facility
  Maintenance and
  Operations
Calgary, AB
B.A.
www.sait.ab.ca

University of Alberta
Physical Education and
Recreation
Edmonton, AB
B.A., M.A.
www.ualberta.ca

University of Calgary
Leisure, Tourism, and Society
Calgary, AB
B.A.
www.ucalgary.ca

University of Calgary
Tourism and Hospitality
Calgary, AB
B.A.
www.ucalgary.ca

University of Lethbridge
Recreation and Leisure
Lethbridge, AB
B.A.
www.uleth.ca

British Columbia

Camosun College
Recreation Leadership
Victoria, BC
Certificate
www.camosun.bc.ca

Capilano College
Outdoor Recreation
Management
North Vancouver, BC
B.A.
www.capcollege.bc.ca

Douglas College
Physical Education,
Recreation, and
Therapeutic Recreation
Greater Vancouver, BC
B.A.
www.douglas.bc.ca

Malaspina University-College
Recreation Administration
and Tourism Studies
Nanaimo, BC
Associates in Recreation
Administration, Tourism
Studies
B.A. in Tourism, Combined
Major Recreation
Administration
www.mala.bc.ca

Selkirk College
Golf Course and Ski Resort
Operations and
Management
Nelson, BC
B.A.
www.selkirk.bc.ca

Selkirk College
Wildland Recreation
Technology
Castlegar, BC
B.A.
www.selkirk.bc.ca

University of British Columbia
Health Science
Vancouver, BC
B.A.
www.ubc.ca

**University College of the
Cariboo**
Tourism and Recreation
Management
Kamloops, BC
B.A.
www.cariboo.bc.ca

**University of Northern British
Columbia**
Resource Recreation and
Tourism Program
Prince George, BC
B.A.
M.A. in Natural Resource
Management
Ph.D. in Natural Resources
Management
www.unbc.ca

University of Victoria
Leisure Studies
Victoria, BC
B.A.
www.uvic.ca

Vancouver Community College
Recreation Leadership and
Facilities Management
Vancouver, BC
Associates
www.vcc.bc.ca

Manitoba

University of Manitoba
Physical Education and
Recreation Studies
Winnepeg, MB
B.A.
www.umanitoba.ca

New Brunswick

Université de Moncton
Physical Education and
    Leisure
Moncton, NB
B.A.
www.umoncton.ca

University of New Brunswick
Physical Education and
    Recreation Faculty
Fredericton, NB
B.A.
www.unb.ca

Newfoundland

**Memorial University of
Newfoundland**
Physical Education and
    Athletics
St. John's, NF
B.A.
www.mun.ca

Northwest Territory

Nunavut Arctic College
Recreation Leaders
Inuvik, NT
Associates
www.nac.nu.ca

Nova Scotia

Acadia University
Recreation Management and
    Kinesiology
Wolfville, NS
B.A., M.A.
www.acadiau.ca

Dalhousie University
Leisure Studies
Halifax, NS
B.A.
www.dal.ca

Ontario

Algonquin College
Recreation and Leisure
    Services Program
Ottawa, ON
B.A.
www.algonquincollege.com

Brock University
Recreation and Leisure
    Studies
St. Catherine's, ON
B.A.
www.brocku.ca

Lakehead University
School of Outdoor
Recreation, Parks, and
Tourism
Thunder Bay, ON
B.A.
www.lakeheadu.ca

Mohawk College
Recreation and Leisure
Services
Hamilton, ON
B.A.
www.mohawkc.on.ca

University of Ottawa
Department of Leisure
Studies
Ottawa, ON
B.A.
www.uottawa.ca

University of Waterloo
Department of Recreation and
Leisure Studies
Waterloo, ON
B.A., M.A.
www.uwaterloo.ca

York University
Wellness Program
York, ON
B.A.
www.yorku.ca

Quebec

Concordia University
Department of Leisure Studies
Montreal, QC
B.A.
www.concordia.ca

Dawson College
Recreation Studies
Westmount, QC
B.A.
www.dawsoncollege.qc.ca

Université du Quebec à Trois-Rivières
Department of Leisure Studies
and Communication
Pavillion Ringuet
Trois-Rivières, QC
B.A. in Recreation
M.A. in Leisure, Culture, and
Tourism
www.uqtr.ca

Saskatchewan

**Saskatchewan Institute of
Applied Science and
Technology**
    Recreation Technology
    Saskatoon, SK
    Associates
    www.siast.sk.ca

University of Regina
    Physical Activity Studies,
        Concentration on
        Recreation Administration
    Regina, SK
    B.A.
    www.uregina.ca

University of Saskatchewan
    Leisure and Sport
        Management Studies
    Saskatoon, SK
    B.A.
    www.usask.ca

Appendix B

Employing Federal and State Agencies

The following federal agencies have major responsibilities in recreation and, therefore, hire recreation personnel. A number of other federal agencies are involved in recreation less extensively and less directly.

Bureau of Land Management
www.blm.gov

Bureau of Reclamation
www.usbr.gov

Department of Agriculture
www.usda.gov

Department of Defense
www.defenselink.mil

Department of Health and Human Services
www.os.dhhs.gov

Department of Housing and Urban Development
www.hud.gov

Department of the Interior
www.doi.gov

Department of Transportation
www.dot.gov

Forest Service
www.fs.fed.us

National Park Service
www.nps.gov

U.S. Army Corps of Engineers
www.usace.army.mil

U.S. Department of Education
www.ed.gov

U.S. Fish and Wildlife Service
www.fws.gov

Even though each state is organized differently, all states have offices that formulate and oversee recreation policy. The following state government divisions typically have recreation and park responsibilities: agriculture, corrections, fisheries and wildlife, forestry, military and veteran affairs, natural resources, state parks, transportation, travel and tourism, and water resources.

Appendix C

Potential Employing Organizations

BECAUSE OF THE diversified nature of leisure activities and leisure occupations, it is not feasible to list all of the employing organizations. But the following list will be helpful:

- Federal government recreation and park related agencies (see Appendix B)
- State government recreation and park related agencies (see Appendix B)
- Municipal, county, and district recreation and park departments
- Community education programs
- Commercial recreation enterprises, such as dude ranches, ski areas, and resorts
- Private clubs for golf, tennis, and swimming
- Recreation and park departments in colleges and universities
- Hospitals and nursing homes with therapeutic recreation programs

- Industrial organizations that sponsor employee recreation
- Correctional institutions
- Professional and service organizations
- Large, youth-serving organizations such as the Boy Scouts, Girl Scouts, Boys Clubs, and Girls Clubs

Appendix D

Professional Organizations

THE FOLLOWING ARE national professional or service organizations that are closely aligned with recreation and parks.

Amateur Athletic Union of
the United States, Inc.
3400 W. Eighty-Sixth St.
Indianapolis, IN 46268
www.aausports.org

Amateur Hockey Association
of the U.S.
2997 Broadmoor Valley Rd.
Colorado Springs, CO 80906

Amateur Softball Association
of America
2801 NE Fiftieth St.
Oklahoma City, OK 73111
www.softball.org

Amateur Trapshooting
Association of America
(ATA)
601 W. National Rd.
Vandalia, OH 45377
www.shootata.com

American Alliance for Health,
Physical Education,
Recreation, and Dance
(AAHPERD)
1900 Association Dr.
Reston, VA 20191-1598
www.aahperd.org

American Alpine Club (AAC)
710 Tenth St., Ste. 100
Golden, CO 80401
www.americanalpineclub.org

American Association of
Botanical Gardens and
Arboreta, Inc. (AABG)
351 Longwood Rd.
Kennett Square, PA 19348-
1807
www.aabga.org

American Association for
Leisure and Recreation
(AALR)
1900 Association Dr.
Reston, VA 20191
www.aapherd.org/aalr/
aalr-main.html

American Association of
Museums
1575 Eye St., Ste. 400
Washington, DC 20005-1105
www.aam-us.org

American Badminton
Association, Inc.
501 W. Sixth St.
Papillion, NE 68046

American Bowling Congress
(ABC)
5301 S. Seventy-Sixth St.
Greendale, WI 53129-1127
www.bowl.org

American Camping
Association (ACA)
5000 State Rd., 67 North
Martinsville, IN 46151-7902
www.aca-camps.org

American Casting Association
1773 Lance End La.
Fenton, MO 63026
www.americancastingassoc.org

American Federation of Arts
41 E. Sixty-Fifth St.
New York, NY 10021
www.afaweb.org

American Folklore Society
(AFS)
4350 N. Fairfax Dr., Ste. 640
Arlington, VA 22203-1620
http://afsnet.org

American Forest and Paper
Association (AF&PA)
1111 Nineteenth St. NW,
Ste. 800
Washington, DC 20036
www.afandpa.org

American Forestry Association
1516 P St. NW
Washington, DC 20005

American Hotel and Motel
Association (National)
(AH&MA)
1201 New York Ave. NW,
Ste. 600
Washington, DC 20005-3931
www.ahma.com

American Motorcycle
Association (AMA)
13515 Yarmouth Dr.
Pickerington, OH 43147
www.ama-cycle.org

American Platform Tennis
Association
Box 43336
Upper Montclair, NJ 07043
www.platformtennis.org

American Running and
Fitness Association
(AR&FA)
4405 East-West Highway,
Ste. 405
Bethesda, MD 20814
www.americanrunning.org

American Society of
Landscape Architects
(ASLA)
636 Eye St. NW
Washington, DC 20001-3736
www.asla.org

American Therapeutic
Recreation Association
(ATRA)
1414 Prince St.
Alexandria, VA 22314
www.atra-tr.org

American Water Ski
  Association (AWSA)
P.O. Box 191
799 Overlook Dr.
Winter Haven, FL 33884
www.usawaterski.org

The American Zoo and
  Aquarium Association
8403 Coleville Rd., Ste. 710
Silver Spring, MD 20910-
  3314
www.aza.org

Antique Automobile Club of
  America, Inc.
501 W. Governor Rd.
Hershey, PA 17033
www.aaca.org

Association for Experiential
  Education (AEE)
2305 Canyon Blvd., Ste. 100
Boulder, CO 80302-5651
www.aee.org

Athletic Institute
200 Castlewood
North Palm Beach, FL 33408

Babe Ruth Baseball Softball
  (BRB)
1770 Brunswick Ave.
P.O. Box 5000
Trenton, NJ 08638
www.baberuthleague.org

Botanical Society of America
  (BSA)
1735 Neil Avenue
Columbus, OH 43210-1293
www.botany.org/bsa

Boy Scouts of America (BSA)
1325 West Walnut Hill La.
P.O. Box 152079
Irving, TX 75015-2079
www.bsa.scouting.org

Boys and Girls Clubs of
  America
1230 W. Peachtree St. NW
Atlanta, GA 30309
www.bgca.org

Camp Fire Boys and Girls
4601 Madison Ave.
Kansas City, MO 64112-1728
www.campfire.org

Club Managers Association of
   America (CMAA)
1733 King St.
Alexandria, VA 22314-2720
www.cmaa.org

Conservation Education
   Association
Oklahoma Conservation
   Commission
2800 Lincoln
Oklahoma City, OK 73105

Conservation Foundation
1250 Twenty-Fourth St. NW
Washington, DC 20037
www.theconservation
   foundation.org

Craft and Hobby Association
319 E. Fifty-Fourth St.
Elmwood Park, NJ 07407
www.hobby.org

Garden Club of America
   (GCA)
14 E. Sixtieth St., FI-3
New York, NY 10022-1006
www.gcamerica.org

Girl Scouts of the United
   States of America
   (GSUSA)
420 Fifth Avenue
New York, NY 10018-2798
www.girlscouts.org

Girls Inc.
120 Wall St., 3rd Fl.
New York, NY 10005-3902
www.girlsinc.org

Hospitality Sales and
   Marketing Association
8201 Greensboro Dr.,
   Ste. 300
McLean, VA 22102
www.hsmai.org

Hostelling International USA
P.O. Box 37613
Washington, DC 20013
www.hiusa.org

Ice Skating Institute (ISI)
17120 Dallas Pkwy., Ste. 140
Dallas, TX 75248
www.skateisi.com

International Association of
Amusement Parks and
Attractions
7222 W. Carnal Dr.
North Riverside, FL 30546
www.iaapa.org

International Association of
Amusement Parks and
Attractions (IAAPA)
4230 King St.
Alexandria, VA 22303
www.iaapa.org

International Association of
Convention and Visitor
Bureaus (IACVB)
2000 L St. NW, Ste. 702
Washington, DC 20036-4990
www.iacvb.org

International Bicycle Touring
Society
P.O. Box 6979
San Diego, CA 92106

International Festivals and
Events Association (IFEA)
115 E. Railroad, Ste. 302
P.O. Box 2950
Port Angeles, WA 98362-
0336
www.ifea.com

International Softball
Congress, Inc.
153 E. 200 S., #10
Farmington, UT 84025
www.iscfastpitch.com

International Spin Fishing
Association
P.O. Box 81
Downey, CA 90241

Izaak Walton League of
America (IWLA)
IWLA Conservation Center
707 Conservation La.
Gaithersburg, MD 20878
www.iwla.org

League of American Bicyclists
1612 K St. NW, Ste. 401
Washington, DC 20006
www.bikeleague.org

Little League Baseball
P.O. Box 3485
Williamsport, PA 17701
www.littleleague.org

Meeting Professionals
International
3030 LBJ Freeway, Ste. 1700
Dallas, TX 75234
www.mpiweb.org

Men's Garden Clubs of
America (GOA)
5560 Merle Hay Rd.
P.O. Box 241
Des Moines, IA 50131-0241
http://dir.gardenweb.com/
directory/tgoamgc

National Amateur Baseball
Federation (NABF)
P.O. Box 705
Bowie, MD 20715
www.nabf.com

National Archery Association
of the U.S. (NAA)
1 Olympic Plaza
Colorado Springs, CO 80909-
5778
www.usarchery.org

National Association of
County Park and
Recreation Officials (NAC)
Genesee County Parks and
Recreation
5045 Stanley Rd.
Flint, MI 48506
www.nacpro.org

National Association of
Intercollegiate Athletics
6120 S.Yale, Ste. 1450
Tulsa, OK 74136
www.naia.org

National Association for
Interpretation
P.O. Box 2246
Fort Collins, CO 80522
www.interpnet.com

National Association of
Professional Forestry
Schools and Colleges
P.O. Box 8001
Raleigh, NC 27695
www.napfsc.org

National Audubon Society
(NAS)
950 Third Ave.
New York, NY 10022
www.audubon.org

National Baseball Congress
(NBC)
Box 1420
Wichita, KA 67201
www.nbcbaseball.com

National Camp Association
(NCA)
610 Fifth Ave.
P.O. Box 5371
New York, NY 10185-5371
www.summercamp.org

National Camping Association
Bradford Woods
Martinsville, IN 46151

National Council for
Therapeutic Recreation
Certification (NCTRC)
7 Elmwood Dr.
New York, NY 10956
www.nctrc.org

National Collegiate Athletic
Association (NCAA)
P.O. Box 6222
700 W. Washington St.
Indianapolis, IN 46206-6222
www.ncaa.org

The National Community
Education Association
3929 Old Lee Highway,
No. 91-A
Fairfax, VA 22030-2401
www.ncea.com

National Duckpin Bowling
Congress (NDBC)
4991 Fairview Ave.
Linthicum Heights, MD
21090
www.ndbc.org

National Field Archery
Association
2407 Outer 1-10
Redlands, CA 92373
www.smart.net/~stimsonr/nfaa
.html

National Garden Clubs, Inc.
4401 Magnolia Ave.
St. Louis, MO 63110-3492
www.gardenclub.org

National Golf Foundation,
Inc.
Rte. 3, Box 210
Hwy. 89 North
Flagstaff, AZ 86004
www.ngf.org

National Industrial Recreation
Association
2400 S. Downing
Westchester, IL 60154

National Institute on Parks
and Grounds Management
(NIPGM)
730 W. Frances St.
Appleton, WI 54913
www.nipgm.org

National Intramural-
Recreational Sports
Association (NIRSA)
4185 SE Research Way
Corvallis, OR 97333-1067
www.nirsa.org

National Junior College
Athletic Association
(NJCAA)
P.O. Box 7305
Colorado Springs, CO 80933-
7305
www.njcaa.org

National Marine
Manufacturers Association
(NMMA)
200 E. Randolph Dr.,
Ste. 5100
Chicago, IL 60601
www.nmma.org

National Model Railroad
Association, Inc. (NMRA)
4121 Cromwell Rd.
Chattanooga, TN 37421
www.nmra.org

National Parks and
Conservation Association
(NPCA)
1300 Nineteenth St. NW
Washington, DC 20036
www.npca.org

National Public Parks Tennis
Association
3325 Wilshire Blvd., Ste. 604
Los Angeles, CA 90010

National Recreation and Parks
Association (NRPA)
22377 Belmont Ridge Rd.
Ashburn, VA 20148
www.nrpa.org

National Rifle Association
(NRA)
11250 Waples Mill Rd.
Fairfax, VA 22030
www.nra.org

National Shuffleboard
Association, Inc.
16900 Slater Rd., #54
Fort Myers, FL 33917-6920
www.geocities.com/national
shuffleboard

National Skeet Shooting
Association (NSSA)
5931 Raft Rd.
San Antonio, TX 78253
www.nssa-nsca.com

National Ski Areas Association
(NSAA)
133 S. Van Gordon, Ste. 300
Lakewood, CO 80228
www.nsaa.org

National Spa and Pool
Institute (NSPI)
2111 Eisenhower Ave.
Alexandria, VA 22314
www.nspi.org

National Therapeutic
Recreation Society
22377 Belmont Ridge Rd.
Ashburn, VA 20148-4501
www.nrpa.org

National Trust for Historic
Preservation (NTHP)
1785 Massachusetts Ave. NW
Washington, DC 20036
www.nationaltrust.org

National Wildlife Federation
(NWF)
8925 Leesburg Pike
Vienna, VA 22184
www.nwf.org

Photographic Society of
America (PSA)
3000 Union Founders Blvd.,
Ste. 103
Oklahoma City, OK 73112
www.psa-photo.org

Pony Baseball and Softball
P.O. Box 225
Washington, PA 15301
www.pony.org

Pop Warner Jr. League
Football
1041 Western Savings Bank
Bldg.
Philadelphia, PA 19107
www.popwarner.com

Professional Rodeo Cowboys
   Association (PRCA)
101 Proprodeo Dr.
Colorado Springs, CO 80919
http://prorodeo.org

Recreation Industrial
   Association
P.O. Box 204
Chantilly, VA 22021

Recreation Vehicle Industry
   Association (RVIA)
1896 Preston White Dr.
P.O. Box 2999
Reston, VA 22090-0999
www.rvia.com

Resort and Commercial
   Recreation Association
   (RCRA)
P.O. Box 1998
Tarpon Springs, FL 34688
www.rcra.org

The Roundtable Associates,
   Inc. (RTA)
404 Highgate Terr.
Silver Springs, MD 20904
www.theroundtableassociates
   .org

Sierra Club
85 Second St., 2nd Fl.
San Francisco, CA
   94109-3441
www.sierraclub.org

Society of American Foresters
   (SAF)
5400 Grosvenor La.
Bethesda, MD 20814
www.safnet.org

Sporting Goods
   Manufacturers Association
   (SGMA)
200 Castlewood Dr.
North Palm Beach, FL 33480
www.sgma.com

Travel Industry Association of
   America (TIAA)
1100 New York Ave. NW,
   Ste. 450
Washington, DC 20005
www.tia.org

United States Lawn Bowls
   Association
1764 N. Fairfax
Los Angeles, CA 90046
www.bowlsamerica.org

U.S. Chess Federation
3054 New York State Rte.9
New Windsor, NY 12553
www.uschess.org

U.S. Equestrian Federation
4047 Iron Works Pkwy.
Lexington, KY 40511
www.usef.org

U.S. Fencing Association
  (USFA)
1 Olympic Plaza
Colorado Springs, CO 80909-
  5744
www.usfencing.org

U.S. Field Hockey Association
1750 E. Boulder St.
Colorado Springs, CO 80909
www.usfieldhockey.com

U.S. Figure Skating
  Association (USFSA)
20 First St.
Colorado Springs, CO 80906
www.usfsa.org

U.S. Golf Association
  (USGA)
P.O. Box 708
Far Hills, NJ 07931
www.usga.org

U.S. Handball Association
930 N. Benton Ave.
Tucson, AZ 85711
www.ushandball.org

U.S. Judo Federation
967 Maybury Ave.
Santa Fe, CA 95133
www.usjf.com

U.S. Parachute Association
1440 Duke St.
Alexandria, VA 22314
www.uspa.org

U.S. Polo Association (USPA)
Kentucky Horse Pkwy., Ste.1
4059 Iron Works Pike
Lexington, KY 40511
www.uspolo.org

US SAILING
P.O. Box 1260
15 Maritime Dr.
Portsmouth, RI 02871
www.ussailing.org

U.S. Squash Racquets
  Association
211 Ford Rd.
Bala Cynwyd, PA 19004
www.us-squash.org/squash

U.S. Tennis Association, Inc.
70 W. Red Oak Ln.
White Plains, NY 10604
www.usta.com

U.S. Volleyball Association
(USVBA)
715 S. Circle Dr.
Colorado Springs, CO 80909-
1740
www.usavolleyball.org

USA Gymnastics
201 S. Capitol
Indianapolis, IN 46225
www.usa-gymnastics.org

USA Table Tennis
1750 E. Boulder St.
Colorado Springs, CO 80909
www.usatt.org

Wilderness Education
Association (WEA)
P.O. Box 158897
Nashville, TN 37215
www.wildernesseducation.org

Wilderness Society
1400 I St. NW
Washington, DC 20005
www.wilderness.org

Wildlife Management
Institute (WMI)
111 Fourteenth St. NW
Washington, DC 20005
www.wildlifemanagement
institute.org

Wildlife Society
5410 Grosvenor La.
Bethesda, MD 20814-2197
www.wildlife.org/index.html

World Tourism Organization
Avenida del Generalissimo 59
Madrid 16
Spain
www.world-tourism.org

Young Men's Christian
Association of the United
States of America (YMCA)
National Council
101 N. Wacker Dr.
Chicago, IL 60606
www.ymca.net

Young Women's Christian
Association of the United
States of America (YWCA)
Empire State Building
350 Fifth Ave., Ste. 301
New York, NY 10118
www.ywca.org

About the Authors

After completing bachelor's and master's degrees and participating in athletic competition at the University of Utah, **Clayne Jensen** completed a three-year term of duty as a commissioned officer in the U.S. Marine Corps. After gaining additional professional experience, he joined the faculty and coaching staff at Utah State University. He worked as a recreation and park specialist for Utah's State Extension Service and was executive director of the State Interagency Council for Recreation, among other teaching and coaching responsibilities.

Professor Jensen completed a doctorate degree at Indiana University in 1963 and has since occupied various teaching and administrative positions at Brigham Young University. He is currently Dean of the College of Health, Physical Education, Recreation, and Athletics. He has also participated extensively in professional organizations, workshops, and conferences. Jensen has established himself as one of the most prolific authors in his field, having authored or coauthored sixteen textbooks, which are currently in print, as well as a large number of professional articles. Because of his achievements, he has received several athletic and professional service awards and has been listed in a number of biographical sources, including *Who's Who in America, Who's Who in Education, Who's Who in the West, International Bibliographies,* and *Men of Achievement.*

Clayne Jensen has remained an avid enthusiast of sports and outdoor recreation and is still both a student and a teacher of active and wholesome activities.

Jay H. Naylor received his B.S. and M.A. degrees in recreation management and physical education from Brigham Young University. He earned his Ed.D. degree from the University of Utah. Naylor's teaching experience has spanned more than twenty-six years at Brigham Young. He served for seven years as Chairman of the Department of Recreation Management and Youth Leadership and is now the associate dean of the college. His professional experience includes work with the Los Angeles Parks and Recreation Department, Spokane Parks and Recreation, and as Director of Pacific Palisades Youth Center in California. He has served as shipboard director of recreation for the Foreign Study League of Salt Lake City, and as Director of the Thames Valley Camp, Ponybourne, England, for the American Camps International. Later he served for two years as a member of the ACI Board of Directors.

Natalia Buta and Amy Decker have revised this edition. Natalia completed her B.S. degree in economics and marketing at the University of Oradea, in Romania. She is currently working on her M.A. degree in recreation, park, and leisure administration at Central Michigan University (CMU), where she is a graduate research assistant. In Romania, Buta was involved with the Romanian Scout Organization for more than seven years. During that time she was a scout leader of a local unit and advanced to a regional facilitator. One of her duties was to aid in improving the educational proposal for the scout program. Upon completion of her master's degree, Natalia hopes to work toward her Ph.D. Then she would like to return to Romania and develop a program at a university to begin educating students about the field of parks, recreation, and tourism.

Amy Decker received her B.A.A. degree from Central Michigan University, majoring in commercial recreation with an emphasis in marketing and communications. She is currently working on her M.A. degree in recreation, park, and leisure administration at CMU. Amy spent five years in event planning and programming with the Michigan Interscholastic Press Association. She left to take an administration internship with the United States Olympic Committee during the 2000 Sydney Olympics. Subsequent opportunities then led her to marketing and communications with the Wharton Center for the Performing Arts, and the Marketing Department for the Detroit Red Wings. Upon completion of her graduate studies, Amy hopes to create and facilitate a nonprofit service organization.